D1646706

Getting the Buggers Fit
(Second Edition)

Also available from Continuum:

Getting the Buggers to Behave (3rd edition) – Sue Cowley

Getting the Buggers to Think (2nd edition) – Sue Cowley

Getting the Buggers to Add Up (2nd edition) – Mike Ollerton

Getting the Buggers into Languages (2nd edition) – Amanda Barton

Getting the Buggers to Write – Sue Cowley

Letting the Buggers be Creative – Sue Cowley

Getting the Buggers to Turn Up – Ian McCormack

Getting the Buggers to do their Homework – Julian Stern

Getting the Buggers to Learn – Duncan Grey

Getting the Buggers to Draw – Barbara Ward

Getting the Buggers into Drama – Sue Cowley

Getting the Buggers into Science – Christine Farmery

Getting the Buggers in Tune – Ian McCormack and Jeanette Healey

Getting the Buggers to Read – Claire Senior

Getting the Buggers to Learn in FE – Angela Steward

Getting the Buggers Motivated in FE – Susan Wallace

Getting the Buggers Fit

Second edition

LORRAINE CALE AND JO HARRIS

continuum

Continuum International Publishing Group

The Tower Building	80 Maiden Lane, Suite 704
11 York Road	New York,
SE1 7NX	NY 10038

www.continuumbooks.com

British Library Cataloguing-in-Publication Data
A catalogue record for this book is available from the British Library.

ISBN: 9780826499790 (paperback)

Library of Congress Cataloging-in-Publication Data
A catalog record for this book is available from the Library of Congress.

Typeset by BookEns Ltd, Royston, Hertfordshire
Printed and bound in Great Britain by MPG Books Ltd, Cornwall

Contents

List of tables   ix

Part I: Why?   1

1   Getting the buggers fit – why bother?   3
Introduction   3
Definitions   5
The health benefits of physical fitness and physical activity   7
Your role and the role of your school   10

**2   Dispelling myths and misunderstandings
and establishing facts**   12
Introduction   12
Activity   12
Children's physical fitness   13
Children's physical activity   17
The activity versus fitness debate   22
References   24
Appendix: Children's fitness, activity and health –
    true and false answers   25

Part II: How? – Understanding Children   27

3   What switches children on and off?   28
Introduction   28
What switches children on and off physical activity?   28
Theories/models used to study correlates of physical
    activity   32
Correlates of physical activity in children   33
Children's sedentary behaviour   36
Common barriers   36
Characteristics of young people   37
Implications   38
Reference   40

4   How often, how hard, how much?   41
Introduction   41

'No gain without pain' – moderate versus vigorous
    physical activity   41
Physical activity recommendations for young people   43
Physical activity recommendations for young people
    in England   44
The government's target for physical activity   45
Issues and recommendations for applying the
    recommendations in practice   47
Implementing and helping your students to
    achieve the recommendations   55
References   56

5   Establishing how fit children are   58
Introduction   58
The purpose of monitoring physical fitness   58
Methods of monitoring physical fitness   59
To test or not to test? – issues   64
Fitness testing recommendations   67
Fitness testing ideas   71
References   80
Appendix: How fit are you?   81

6   Establishing how active children are   86
Introduction   86
The purpose of monitoring physical activity   86
Methods of monitoring physical activity   87
Implementing physical activity monitoring with
    your students   91
Using the physical activity information   101
Alternative monitoring methods   102

Part III: How? – The Curriculum   105

7   The physical education curriculum   107
Introduction   107
Developments   107
HRE interpretation and philosophy   116
References   121

8   Other physical education curriculum issues   122
Introduction   122
Status and time   122
Teacher knowledge, understanding and attitudes   123

Links to other curriculum areas 124
Research developments 131
Making physical activity and sport relevant and
attractive to children 133
Time for reflection 136
References 136

9 **Physical activity, physical education and
childhood obesity** 138
Introduction 138
Definition, facts and figures 138
Associated health problems 139
Factors contributing to obesity 140
The importance of physical activity and physical
activity promotion to obese children 141
Promoting physical activity to obese children 142
Guidance and recommendations 145
General and activity recommendations 147
References 152

Part IV: How? The Whole School 153

10 **Whole-school approaches** 155
Introduction 155
Whole-school approaches 156
The Healthy School 157
The Active School 159
Final recommendations 161
References 163

11 **Challenges and solutions** 164
Introduction 164
Common issues 164
Recommended practical steps and procedures 166
Solutions and strategies 171
Ideas for physical activity and sports promotional events 181
Practical tips for implementing strategies 183
Guidelines for establishing an Active School Committee 184
Guidelines for monitoring and evaluation 185

12 **Real-life examples** 188
Introduction 188
Case studies 189
References 196

Part Five: How? – Beyond the School   197

13 **Opportunities and support**   199
    Introduction   199
    Government strategies and associated initiatives   200
    Non-government initiatives   207
    Useful resources, websites and contacts   211
    Points to note   215
    Recommendations   217
    Concluding remarks   218
    Reference   218

    Index   219

List of Tables

Table 2.1   A summary of the key points and findings
            concerning children's fitness   15
Table 2.2   A summary of the key findings and trends
            concerning children's physical activity   18
Table 3.1   The correlates of children's physical activity (PA)   30
Table 3.2   Issues and implications or recommendations   38
Table 4.1   Recommendations for strength and flexibility
            exercises with children   52
Table 4.2   Ideas for implementing the recommendations
Table 5.1   A summary of some of the more common field
            tests of physical fitness for children   55
Table 5.2   A summary of the advantages and disadvantages
            of norm- and criterion-referenced standards   60
Table 5.3   Recommendations for fitness testing with children   63
Table 6.1   Physical activity monitoring methods and their
            main strengths and limitations   68
Table 7.1   The Key HRE Requirements of the New Secondary
            NCPE – Key Stage 3   89
Table 7.2   The Key HRE Requirements of the New Secondary
            NCPE – Key Stage 4   109
Table 7.3   The approaches to delivering HRE
Table 8.1   HRE within the National Curriculum at Key
            Stage 3: Physical Education, Personal, Social and
            Health Education: Personal Wellbeing, Science and
            Design and Technology   125
Table 8.2   HRE within the National Curriculum at Key
            Stage 4: Physical Education, Personal, Social and
            Health Education: Personal Wellbeing and Science   127
Table 9.1   NICE obesity guidance for schools   146
Table 9.2   Recommendations for physical education teachers
            for addressing childhood obesity   149
Table 10.1 Example Active School Policy   160
Table 13.1 Useful resources   212
Table 13.2 Relevant teacher and student web sites   213
Table 13.3 Useful contact organizations and their websites   214

I | Why?

Introduction

Concerns over children's fitness and the notion that we need to 'get the buggers fit' are not new but have attracted particular interest from government ministers, health practitioners, educationalists, researchers and the media in recent years. A great deal of media attention and 'hype' has been given to the issue of children's fitness, with common messages being that most youngsters today are unfit and far less fit than in the past. At the same time, even greater attention and hype has been afforded to the growing levels of fatness and obesity in young people, with perhaps inevitably links being made between the two. Some have described the issues as 'growing epidemics'. Also, the view that there are links between children's fitness and their health, and more recently, between fitness and fatness both in childhood and adulthood are common. In other words, it is thought 'fit' children are healthier and thinner, and grow up to be healthier and thinner adults.

It is perhaps as a result of the concerns over children's fitness (and possibly fatness) and the likely health consequences that the teaching of 'health and fitness' within schools and as part of the physical education curriculum is now commonplace. The National Curriculum for Physical Education provides a clear and strong emphasis on health-related issues within physical education, further enhancing its popularity and status. Indeed, alarmed by media reports and the statutory requirements they are required to meet, many schools and physical education teachers today may feel pressured, forced and even duty bound to respond by focusing on and trying to improve children's fitness.

The title of this book focuses on fitness, but as we go on to reveal in the following two chapters, and contrary to popular belief, children's fitness levels do not tell a wholly accurate story. In fact, they tell us very little about children's health or lifestyles. Of greater importance to children's health is how much physical activity they do. Yet, there are similar concerns about young people's physical activity. The youth of today have been described as 'couch kids' and there are fears over their low and decreasing levels of physical activity. We perhaps only have to observe the lifestyle and habits of Harry Enfield's teenage character 'Kevin', or the behaviour and attitude of Catherine Tate's modern-day school girl 'Lauren', to appreciate some of the problems. Kevin is addicted to TV watching, computer games, labour-saving gadgets and junk food. He is taxied everywhere by his devoted and 'over-protective' parents and will go to great lengths to escape 'active' chores such as tidying his room or washing the car! He does of course own a pair of trainers, but these are merely a fashion accessory – their only wear and tear comes from being dragged along the floor as he walks. Even picking up his feet is too much of a physical effort for the tiresome teenager. Lauren, on the other hand, is more independent, but her characteristic 'am I bovvered?' attitude means she is lazy, disinterested, bored and unimpressed by most things, and especially, it seems, by what school has to offer. She furthermore readily challenges authority and order and thereby says and does exactly what she wants. Thus, while her tongue is usually very active, the rest of her certainly is not. Although it could be argued that such behaviours and attitudes are 'typical' of teenagers from any generation, there is no doubt that the pressures upon and the opportunities and choices for Kevin and Lauren as young people growing up in today's society to be sedentary and/or simply opt out of physical activity are very real.

In this book, we explore children's physical fitness and physical activity and the key issues and implications for teachers. In short, we consider what you, as a physical education teacher, can do to try to 'get the buggers' more fit and active! First, we provide relevant background information to help explain *why* we need to bother getting children fit and active, by looking at the health benefits of physical fitness and physical activity. We hope that you will share this information with senior management, colleagues, parents and students. Then, we present a range of practical ideas, strategies and tips as to *how* we might get youngsters fit and active. In so doing, we look at the promotion of healthy, active lifestyles in schools as the way to improve children's fitness and activity. The reason for focusing on active lifestyles is explained in Chapter 2. In addition, and given the growing interest and concerns over childhood obesity, we consider the role physical activity and physical education can play in addressing the issue.

In summary, within the book we aim to provide you with answers to the following questions:

- How important is physical fitness and physical activity to children's health?
- How physically fit and active are children?
- How much physical activity should children do?
- How can you monitor your students' physical fitness and physical activity?
- What influences children's physical activity participation?
- How can you, your department and school promote healthy, active lifestyles to your students?
- What role can physical activity, physical education and you play in addressing childhood obesity?
- What ideas, initiatives and strategies are possible and available to support your efforts to promote healthy, active lifestyles among your students?
- What resources, websites and contacts are available to support your efforts to promote healthy, active lifestyles among your students?

Within this book, we take a brief look at some theory but only in so far as it should affect and inform your practice. We make no apologies for this, as we firmly believe that if your efforts to influence your students are to be successful, then they need to be based on an awareness and understanding of the key facts and issues. In fact, this theory is not only relevant for yourself, but at the appropriate level, should be shared with your students as well.

Following an introduction to key terms used in the book, in this chapter we look at the importance of physical fitness and physical activity to children's health, and then consider your role and that of your school and department in promoting healthy, active lifestyles.

Definitions

On the following pages we provide definitions for some of the key terms that are used within the book.

Adolescence – Adolescence is sometimes used to refer to the psychological changes associated with puberty. Within this text however, adolescence and puberty are assumed to be synonymous and refer to the period during which a young person experiences the somatic, physical and psychological changes that occur as they develop into adults.

Childhood – The period from the first birthday to the onset of puberty.

Exercise – A sub-component of physical activity which is volitional, planned, structured, repetitive and carried out to improve or maintain any aspect of fitness or health.

Health – A state of complete physical, mental and social well-being and not merely the absence of disease or infirmity. It is a resource for everyday life and a positive concept emphasizing social and personal resources, as well as physical capacities.

Health promotion – All measures deliberately designed to promote health. It includes health education, plus healthy public policy which aims to achieve social change via legislation, economic and other forms of environmental engineering. It is concerned with making 'healthier' choices, 'easier' choices.

Health-related exercise – The area of the physical education curriculum associated with health and fitness. Health-related exercise is physical activity associated with health enhancement and involves the teaching of knowledge, understanding, physical competence and behavioural skills, and the creation of positive attitudes and confidence associated with current and lifelong participation in physical activity.

Obesity – Obesity is a clinical term for a condition that is characterized by an excessive amount of body fat. Obesity can result in a significant impairment of health and is associated with an increased risk of illness, disability and death.

Overweight – This is a clinical term that implies higher than normal levels of body fat and more than is considered normal or healthy for one's age or build.

Physical activity – A broad term that refers to any bodily movement produced by skeletal muscles that uses energy. It has dimensions of volume (how much), duration (how long), frequency (how often), intensity (how hard) and mode (what type). The latter encompasses physical education and sport, active play and routine, habitual activities such as walking and cycling, as well as housework and gardening.

Physical activity promotion – All measures deliberately designed to promote physical activity. It includes health education, plus healthy public policy which aims to achieve social change via legislation, economic and other forms of environmental engineering. It is concerned with making 'active' choices, 'easier' choices.

Physical education – The planned, progressive learning that takes place in school curriculum timetabled time and which is delivered to all students. This involves both 'learning to move' (i.e. becoming more physically competent) and 'moving to learn' (e.g. learning through movement, a range of skills and understandings beyond physical activity such as co-operating with others). The context for the learning is physical activity, with children experiencing a broad range of activities, including sport and dance.

Physical fitness – A set of attributes that a person has or achieves that relates to the ability to perform physical activity. Physical fitness has health-related components and performance (skill)-related components. The health-related components of physical fitness include cardiovascular fitness, muscular strength and endurance, flexibility and body composition. The performance-related aspects include agility, balance, co-ordination, power, reaction time and speed. This type of fitness is also sometimes referred to as motor fitness.

Sport – A sub-component of exercise that is rule governed, structured and competitive and involves gross motor movement characterized by physical strategy, prowess and chance.

School sport – This is the structured learning that takes place beyond the school curriculum (i.e. in the extended curriculum), sometimes referred to as out-of-school-hours learning. The context for the learning is physical activity. The 'school sport' programme has the potential to develop and broaden the foundation learning that takes place in physical education. It also forms a vital link with 'community sport and activity'.

Young people – All people aged 5 to 18 years.

The health benefits of physical fitness and physical activity

Evidence on the benefits of physical activity and physical fitness to children's health is growing and has been the focus of much research over the past decade. However, in contrast to adults, still relatively little is known about children's fitness, activity and the associated health benefits.

We know that participation in regular physical activity can have a number of health benefits for children. A comprehensive review of the research in this area reveals these to include the following:

Psychological well-being – Physical activity can help young people feel better about themselves and reduce symptoms of depression and anxiety.

Self-esteem – Physical activity can result in increased self-confidence and self-worth. This is particularly the case in disadvantaged groups such as those with learning difficulties and those with initially low self-esteem.

Moral and social development – If appropriately structured, physical activity may improve young people's ability to relate to others, as well as their sense of fair play and justice.

Avoiding being overweight and obesity – There are small but significant beneficial effects of increased physical activity on reducing body fat. Evidence supports the role of physical activity as part of an effective obesity treatment for young people, when combined with appropriate dietary modification.

Reduced chronic disease risk factors – Physical activity has a small beneficial association with serum lipid and lipoprotein concentrations and blood pressure. Recent research has also identified a favourable relationship between physical activity and a range of factors associated with metabolic syndromes (e.g. hypertension, obesity, insulin resistance, impaired lipid and lipoprotein profile). In addition, weight bearing and strength-enhancing physical activity can promote skeletal health in young people.

The latter two benefits are particularly important given reports of increased rates of overweight and obesity in children and the associated health problems, and given that we know cardiovascular disease (CVD) has its origins in childhood. Evidence is also mounting to support the benefits of physical fitness to children. For example, there is firm scientific evidence that physical fitness is related to a healthy CVD risk profile and body fatness in children and adolescents, and some evidence that it may have a positive influence on psychological health.

There is some uncertainty however, as to whether childhood physical activity and/or physical fitness influence health in later life. There is no strong evidence that physical activity and/or physical fitness during childhood and adolescence are related to CVD risk factors in adulthood, or to the occurrence of CVD in adulthood. Despite this, the evidence that fitness influences future health is becoming more and more persuasive and is stronger than for physical activity. Findings from a few large-scale studies have suggested that high physical fitness during adolescence and young adulthood is related to a healthy risk factor profile later in life. The same findings suggest that physical activity levels during adolescence and young adulthood do not influence CVD risk in later life.

However, this association may in part be genetically determined and be independent of activity. For instance, a high fit individual could automatically be blessed with better health and a low fit individual could be unfortunate to have poorer health. Another explanation might be that high levels of fitness encourage higher activity, which might improve cardiovascular health and other health indicators (e.g. lower blood pressure).

Summary
Many people are often surprised that the health benefits of physical fitness and physical activity in children are not better established, and that some of the benefits and links between physical activity and physical fitness appear to be only small or relatively weak. Certainly, the clear associations between health, physical activity and physical fitness that are seen in adults have yet to be confirmed in children. However, there are a number of reasons that might explain why the evidence is not stronger or more convincing. For example:

◆ There is a lack of large-scale longitudinal studies conducted on children.
◆ There are numerous difficulties in measuring children's health, fitness and activity (see Chapters 5 and 6).
◆ Many studies have investigated the relationship of sustained vigorous activity or exercise training to children's health, but as Chapter 2 reveals, children do not tend to engage in this kind of activity.
◆ Children's health cannot be measured by mortality statistics as it is in adults. Instead, traditional CVD risk factors are usually relied upon which are only a crude indicator of cardiovascular health.
◆ For many children, it is likely that their habit of a physically inactive lifestyle has had insufficient time to negatively influence such risk factors.

◆ Insufficient numbers of children may be inactive for the negative health consequences to be seen (see Chapter 2).

To summarize, given (i) the strong relationships between fitness or activity and health in adults; (ii) the growing evidence for these relationships in children; (iii) that CVD has its origins in childhood; and (iv) the increased rates of obesity and other associated health conditions in children, it would seem common sense for us to conclude that adequate physical fitness and physical activity are indeed important and provide real benefits to all young people.

Your role and the role of your school

Schools are often seen as the most important avenue through which to promote children's healthy, active lifestyles and school physical education and physical education teachers in particular are recognized as having a key and almost 'taken for granted' role to play. Health and physical activity promotion is now a widely accepted goal of physical education. But why? Quite simply, your school:

◆ provides a captive audience and access to all your students;
◆ occupies a good deal of your students' time and can influence their behaviour for about 40 to 45 per cent of their waking time;
◆ can potentially influence not only your students, but adults (including teachers, teaching assistants, ancillary staff, governors and parents) as well;
◆ through physical education (and personal, social and health education) has the appropriate knowledge and expertise (that of yourself and colleagues!);
◆ through physical education can potentially raise awareness, set expectations and develop knowledge, confidence and positive attitudes in your students with respect to health and physical activity;
◆ has a statutory responsibility 'to provide a balanced and broadly based curriculum which promotes the spiritual, moral, cultural, mental and *physical* development of learners' (2002 Education Act).

Furthermore, through health-related physical education programmes, schools have been shown to be successful in the past and to positively influence children's physical fitness, physical activity and dietary behaviours, and their knowledge and attitudes towards physical activity and/or physical education.

Finally, the role of schools and physical education in promoting health, the link between health and education, and encouraging participation in sport and physical activity have been increasingly recognized and have become a focus of government policy in recent years. Every Child Matters, for example, is concerned with the well-being of young people, a key outcome of which is to support children to 'be healthy', whilst the Physical Education and Sport Strategy for Young People (formerly the Physical Education, School Sport and Club Links Strategy), focuses on increasing participation in sport and physical activity. Further details about this Strategy are provided in Chapter 13.

As a result, it would seem important that you, your colleagues and your school not only recognize your role and the expectations upon you, but know *how* to go about promoting healthy, active lifestyles among your students and thereby influence their physical fitness, physical activity and overall health and well-being. We hope to help you to achieve this in the following chapters of this book.

2 | Dispelling myths and misunderstandings and establishing facts

Introduction

As we highlighted in Chapter 1, there has been considerable interest in and concern over children's physical fitness and physical activity levels in recent years. Yet, while many of us might have stories to share to illustrate how unfit, inactive and consequently unhealthy the youth of today are, there is in fact relatively limited 'hard' evidence to confirm this picture. A number of myths and misunderstandings have developed concerning children's physical fitness and physical activity over the years, often reinforced by the popular media. Evidently, if you are to be successful in your efforts to influence either, you need to be clear from the start what the key facts, issues and messages are and/or should be. Your task should then be to dispel the myths and misunderstandings among colleagues, parents and your students. In this chapter, we summarize the key messages and findings from the research available to clarify the facts about children's physical fitness and physical activity.

Activity

Before reading on, complete this short task to determine what you currently know about children's fitness, activity and health.

Read the following statements and establish which you think are true (T), and which you think are false (F). The answers to the first few statements have already been provided in Chapter 1. Then, study this chapter and check your answers with the Table in the Appendix to this chapter. Were you as well informed as you thought?

Statement T or F?

- The onset of cardiovascular disease begins in childhood.
- There is overwhelmingly strong evidence that physical activity is beneficial to children's health.
- Physical activity has been found to benefit some chronic disease risk factors, body fatness, skeletal health and psychological well-being in young people.
- Childhood overweight and obesity is neither increasing nor decreasing in the UK.
- Children's aerobic fitness generally increases with age.
- Some children are very active whereas others are very inactive.
- There is a good deal of evidence that children today are less fit than in the past.
- Low aerobic fitness is common among children.
- A sizeable proportion of children in the UK are inactive and lead sedentary lifestyles.
- Girls are more active than boys.
- Physical activity levels increase with age, with the teenage years being the most active time.
- People who are active during childhood are more likely to be active in adulthood.
- Children are generally the fittest and most active group of the population.
- Most boys and girls are not fit enough to benefit their health.

Children's physical fitness

National fitness survey findings

Large-scale national fitness surveys have been conducted in the United Kingdom (UK) and elsewhere, for example, in Northern Ireland, the United States (US), Canada and Australia, but this was primarily during the 1980s. These included the Northern Ireland Fitness Survey (1989), The National Children and Youth Fitness Studies I and 2 (1985, 1987), The President's Council on Physical Fitness and Sports National School Population Survey (1985), The Canada Fitness Survey (1981), The

Campbell Survey on Well Being in Canada (1988) and the Australian Health and Fitness Survey (1985). Although there have been a number of regional and more local surveys and studies of children's fitness since this time, there have been no further national surveys. Below we present a summary of some of the key observations and findings which stem from these surveys.

With respect to the national fitness surveys, we feel the following points are worthy of note.

1. While the surveys were often referred to as 'fitness' surveys, this title was in fact somewhat misleading as each addressed more than simply fitness. Physical activity participation was also surveyed within the studies.
2. Other elements of the surveys included measures of lifestyle generally (e.g. smoking, drinking, dietary habits), as well as attitudes towards physical activity, exercise and sport.
3. Limitations in the methods and test items that were used in these surveys have been widely reported (see Chapter 5 for details).
4. In terms of fitness, average scores on various fitness test items tended to be reported, with no interpretation of their meaning and/or implications for children's health, and with few firm or definitive conclusions drawn concerning the fitness status of children. In our view, the practical value and use of such surveys is therefore limited.

Other fitness study findings

Further details we have concerning children's physical fitness have come from national and international field-based studies or surveys conducted at a regional or local level, as well as from laboratory-based studies of children's fitness. In the laboratory, maximal oxygen uptake, or the highest rate at which an individual can utilize oxygen during exercise, limits the capacity to perform aerobic exercise and is therefore recognized to be the best measure of children's aerobic fitness. It is determined by collecting and analysing expired air samples during a maximal exercise test, usually on a treadmill or cycle ergometer. The first studies to measure children's aerobic fitness by this method were conducted between 50 and 65 years ago, but now the method is frequently used. In the field, physical fitness is measured according to performance on a range of fitness tests designed to assess different components of fitness.

Again, we have summarized some of the key points and consistent findings from laboratory- and field-based children's fitness studies for you (see Table 2.1). When scrutinizing these however, it should be borne in mind that studies and hence the evidence are still relatively limited. Furthermore, the studies often provide only local snapshots and are restricted to particular age groups and fitness components (usually aerobic fitness).

Are today's children unfit and less fit?
It is perhaps the latter few findings in Table 2.1 that might be a surprise and seem rather confusing. For a number of years now it has been widely reported in the media that children are unfit, and/or that they are less fit than in previous generations. However, there is in fact scarce evidence to support the former view, and equivocal or contradictory evidence to support the latter.

Table 2.1 A summary of the key points and findings concerning children's fitness

Summary of Key Points and Findings

◆ Children show a progressive, almost linear increase in aerobic fitness with age, although from about 14 years, girls' aerobic fitness seems to level off.

◆ Boys' aerobic fitness increases through childhood and adolescence and into early adulthood, whereas girls' increases into puberty before levelling off.

◆ Boys' aerobic fitness is higher than girls' at least from late childhood, with the difference between boys' and girls' becoming greater during the teenage years.

◆ Within Europe, there is considerable variation in children's performance on fitness tests but children from northern (e.g. Finland, Iceland, Estonia) and central European countries (Slovakia, Czech Republic) have been found to perform the best.

◆ There is no firm evidence to suggest that low levels of aerobic fitness are common among children.

◆ Evidence supporting any particular trend (e.g. consistent or downward) in children's aerobic fitness over time is equivocal or contradictory. Laboratory-based studies suggest that children's aerobic fitness has not changed over the last 50 years, while some recent evidence based on field tests suggests that children's aerobic performance has declined over the past 30 years.

◆ There is some recent evidence to suggest a 'polarization' in children's aerobic fitness (which is where there are extremes of fit and unfit children), is emerging, with the difference increasing over time.

On the issue of whether children are fit enough, there is no actual agreement with respect to the 'optimal' level of physical fitness for young people. In other words, nobody knows for sure how fit children should be for their health. Despite this, experts have suggested that it may be possible to express a lower limit of aerobic fitness, or a threshold level, below which may represent a 'health risk'. Although few studies have reported data in sufficient detail to estimate the number of children falling below this level, a re-analysis of the aerobic fitness of over 3,000 young people tested over the last 15 years by Professor Armstrong and colleagues at the Children's Exercise and Health Research Centre at Exeter University, revealed that less than 2 per cent of children fell below the proposed 'health risk' threshold (Armstrong, 2004). Furthermore, if the average values obtained in longitudinal studies of aerobic fitness on children are considered, these quite comfortably exceed the health-risk threshold values.

Similarly in the US, 'healthy fitness zone' criteria (standards specifying the minimum levels of fitness thought to be required for health) have been proposed for field-based tests across different components of fitness which, based on the available data, have been used to summarize the physical fitness status of children (Malina, 2007). The summary revealed that the majority of children met or exceeded the criterion-referenced 'healthy fitness zone' standards. On this basis, it was suggested that generalizations about the 'fitness or unfitness' of children need to be made with caution and that the level of children's health-related physical fitness seems acceptable.

Whether children have become less fit over the years is another interesting topic of debate, and opinion seems to be more divided on this issue. Based on an analysis of data over almost six decades at Exeter University, Professor Armstrong and colleagues concluded that the aerobic fitness of young people who volunteer for fitness tests has not changed over the last 50 years (Armstrong and Fawkner, 2007). They tell us that the aerobic fitness of children appears to have remained remarkably consistent over time, with the fitness scores of children today being very similar to those reported decades ago.

In contrast, since 1970, data from performance tests have consistently indicated a decrease in children's aerobic fitness. A recent review of 33 studies of children's aerobic fitness from 27 countries over a 45-year period reported a global decline in children's aerobic performance (Tomkinson and Olds, 2007). This decrease, however, could be due to a number of reasons and it is plausible that it may be a reflection of the rise in children's body mass over time rather than a true reduction in fitness. Regardless, it seems that the increase in children's body mass is not being accompanied by a corresponding increase in their aerobic fitness, with the inevitable result being that, in activities which involve moving body mass, children's aerobic performance is declining.

Thus, in summary, there appears to be no firm evidence to suggest that low levels of aerobic fitness are common among children, and equivocal or contradictory evidence concerning whether children's fitness has declined over the years or not. What is perhaps of some concern and worthy of note however, is the reported 'polarization' of children's aerobic fitness levels, with a clear gap between the least and most fit children. At the same time though, we should bear in mind that there are many limitations with fitness testing and fitness data and many factors influence fitness test scores. We discuss the limitations and issues concerning fitness testing of children in Chapter 5.

Children's physical activity

Information about children's physical activity levels has frequently been reported, particularly in the UK, US and Europe. Despite this, and due often to the different types of physical activity information collected and the different methods used (see Chapter 6 for details on methods of monitoring physical activity), the reports are often mixed with sometimes quite contrasting pictures and conclusions drawn concerning how active or inactive children are. Nonetheless, we are able to identify a number of key findings and consistent trends from the research with some confidence. We have drawn these from findings from reviews, and large-scale international and UK-based studies (see Table 2.2).

As with physical fitness, the numerous studies and reviews from which we have summarized the findings in Table 2.2 are not described. However, we provide summary details of some of the recent large-scale studies which have been conducted on young people's physical activity in the UK. It would be interesting to compare these findings with the activity levels of your students (see Chapter 6 for ideas on how to do this). Also, we feel the debate over whether children's physical activity has decreased in recent years is likely to be of interest and deserves attention.

Table 2.2 A summary of the key findings and trends concerning children's physical activity

Summary of Key Findings and Trends

♦ In the UK, recent surveys suggest that three in ten boys and four in ten girls fail to meet physical activity recommendations for young people (see Chapter 4), which means that a sizeable proportion of children are inactive and lead sedentary lifestyles.

♦ National and international surveys reveal relatively good levels of participation, particularly in organized sport, among a significant proportion of children.

♦ 'Polarization' of activity (where there are extreme groups of very active and very inactive individuals), appears to be common in children.

♦ Boys are more active than girls and the difference is more marked in vigorous activity.

♦ Physical activity decreases with age with the teenage years being the time of greatest decline.

♦ Children's physical activity patterns appear to be sporadic and highly transitory or changeable, with sustained periods of moderate to vigorous physical activity not being part of most children's lifestyles.

♦ There is some evidence, albeit limited, that children's activity and inactivity tracks from childhood to adulthood – in other words, that active children are more likely to remain and become active adults and vice versa.

Large-scale surveys on children's physical activity in the UK

The Health Survey for England (2006)

The Health Survey for England has involved children aged 2 to 15 since 1995, and the 2006 Health Survey included a focus on childhood obesity and other risk factors for children, including physical activity. A total of 7,257 children were included in the sample and questions were asked about out-of-school participation across four activity categories: (i) sports and exercise, (ii) active play, (iii) walking and (iv) housework/gardening.

The findings revealed that 95 per cent of boys and 92 per cent of girls had participated in some physical activity on five or more days in the last week. The most common activity for boys was active play, followed by walking, and for girls, walking followed by active play. Overall, boys spent an average of 13.8 hours and girls an average of 10.9 hours in the last week being physically active. Participation in sports and exercise specifically however, was lower, with 22 per cent of boys and 14 per cent of girls taking part on at least five days. Seven in ten boys and six in ten girls met the current physical activity recommendations for children (i.e. participated in physical activity of at least moderate intensity for 60 minutes or more every day in the preceding week) (see Chapter 4). Among girls, the time spent participating in physical activity decreased with age (from 2 to 15 years), while among boys the time spent remained at a similar level throughout childhood.

These findings compare favourably against the 1997 Health Survey for England findings when physical activity was included for the first time. This earlier survey revealed 78 per cent of boys and 70 per cent of girls to have participated in some physical activity on five or more days, and boys to spend an average of 10.41 hours and girls 7.69 hours during the last week in physical activities.

Sport England's Young People and Sport National Surveys

Three national Surveys of Young People and Sport in England have been conducted for Sport England in 1994, 1999, and most recently in 2002. The surveys involved over 3,000 young people aged 6 to 16 and provided information on their participation in sport in school lessons, in extracurricular activities and in their leisure time, as well as about their attitudes towards sport.

With regard to sport outside of school lessons, the surveys revealed almost all young people to have taken part in some sporting activity at least once in the previous 12 months, with the figure remaining unchanged since 1994. At the same time though, a significant minority (around 13 to 14 per cent) were found not to take part in any sport regularly in their free time. The top three sports played regularly outside of lessons remained the same between 1994 and 2002, these being swimming, cycling and football.

While the surveys revealed the amount of time spent on sport out of lessons to have remained fairly consistent, they did report increased participation in extracurricular sport (40 per cent in 2002 compared with approximately a third in 1994), as well as fewer young people spending less than one hour, or no time, in a week doing sports or exercise in 2002 than was the case in 1994. A slight increase from 1994 to 2002 was also reported in the proportion of young people spending five or more, or ten or more hours of sports and exercise per week during the summer holidays.

Taking Part Survey (2006)
The Taking Part Survey was commissioned by the Department for Culture, Media and Sport and collected data about engagement in culture, leisure and sport. There was a children's element to the 2006 survey which involved interviewing approximately 3,000 11 to 15 year olds about their engagement in activities during the last 12 months and their patterns of engagement out of school lessons. This included break time, lunch time, after school, at the weekend and during school holidays.

Findings from the child survey revealed that 95 per cent of children had engaged in an active sport during the last four weeks. Of those, 93 per cent had participated in an active sport out of school lessons (which equated to 89 per cent of all children). In terms of frequency, approximately three quarters of all children had participated in an active sport outside school lessons in the last week and, of those, nearly a quarter had participated for at least an hour on one day, a fifth had participated for at least an hour on two days, and around a quarter had participated for at least an hour on five or more days. The most common active sports participated in were football, followed by swimming or diving (both in and out of lessons), and basketball (in lessons) or cycling (out of lessons).

The 2006/2007 School Sport Survey
The 2006/2007 School Sport Survey was commissioned by the Department for Children, Schools and Families. It represents the fourth survey to be conducted among schools involved in the School Sport Partnership Programme through the Physical Education and Sport Strategy for Young People (formerly the Physical Education, School Sport and Club Links Strategy) (see Chapter 13 for details). The survey collected information about levels of participation in physical education and school sport from 21,745 partnership schools. Whilst the sample was not therefore representative of all schools, and the data were not collected by trained researchers, the survey nonetheless revealed some interesting findings.

The survey reported that overall 86 per cent of pupils in schools within the School Sport Partnership Programme participated in at least two hours of high quality physical education and out-of-hours school sport in a typical week. There were however, clear differences in levels of participation between primary and secondary schools and year groups, with levels of participation being higher in primary (91 per cent) than in secondary schools (80 per cent), and noticeably lower in years 10 and 11

(67 and 63 per cent respectively). Compared to the previous surveys, participation in at least two hours of physical education and school sport was reported to have increased from 62 per cent in the first survey in 2003/04, to 86 per cent in the 2006/07 survey, with the most marked improvements in participation being found in the primary schools. Participation levels in years 10 and 11 were consistently recorded at a low level and showed only small improvements.

In terms of participation in intra- and inter-school competitive activities, aside from school sports days, 58 per cent of pupils in partnership schools were reported to be involved in intra-school sports activities and 35 per cent were involved in inter-school competition during the academic year. Participation in the latter furthermore showed a 7 per cent increase from the first to the fourth survey.

Are today's children less active?

As with fitness, a common belief and one that has often been reported in the media is that children today are less active than they were in the past. But in fact, we cannot categorically say whether children's physical activity has declined in recent years or not. To determine this, physical activity information must be collected from studies over a period of time that have used the same methods with similar groups of children, but such studies are virtually non-existent.

However, some studies throw some light on this matter. One study, for example, provides indirect evidence to support the claim that activity levels have decreased. A study of children's eating habits analysed data collected over 50 years (from the 1930s–80s) and showed that there had been a steady decrease in the energy or food intake of adolescents in the UK, but no change in their body weight over time (Durnin, 1992). The only feasible explanation that can be given for the marked reduction in energy intake without a change in body weight is that children's physical activity decreased over the 50 year period.

Further indications of a decrease in children's activity levels come if we look at changes in children's lifestyles and travel patterns over time. Children now spend more time watching television and engaged in other sedentary activities such as playing computer games. Indeed, it has been reported that British children currently spend 55 per cent of their waking lives in front of televisions and computers, devoting on average five hours a day to these types of activities. In addition, parents place more restrictions on children these days and their freedom to be independently active has decreased quite dramatically in recent years. For example, the Taking Part Survey (2007) mentioned earlier revealed that 45 per cent of adults do not allow their children to play outside, with one of the most frequently given reasons being that it is too dangerous. This perhaps also explains why fewer children now walk or cycle to school. Since the early 1990s there has been a steady decrease in the number of children walking and cycling to school in the UK, with the proportion of children aged 5 to 10 who walk to school having fallen from 61 per cent in the early 1990s, to 52 per cent in 2006. The proportion of 11 to 16 year olds walking to school is 41 per cent and just 1 per cent of 5 to 10 year olds and 3 per cent of 11 to 16 year olds now cycle to school. Such changes must have led to decreases in the physical activity levels of many children.

More recently though, some studies, in which data were compared over relatively shorter periods of time (e.g. over five to ten years), have suggested a consistent or even an upward trend in children's physical activity levels. For example, a study conducted at Exeter University concluded that activity levels had not fallen dramatically over the period of a decade (Welsman and Armstrong, 2000). In addition, the surveys outlined earlier such as the Health Survey for England, the Sport England Young People and Sport Surveys, and the School Sport Surveys have generally reported increased participation rates over time.

As we warned was the case when considering the children's fitness data, there are similarly limitations with physical activity monitoring and with physical activity data that need to be borne in mind. Such limitations make it impossible to firmly establish whether children today are less active, as active, or indeed more active than they have been in the past. Whilst children's activity levels may have decreased over previous generations, certainly if we accept the figures from recent surveys then it seems the picture may well now be improving. Perhaps recent commitment and financial investment by the government in physical education and school sport through the Physical Education and Sport Strategy for Young People (formerly the Physical Education, Schools Sport and Club Links) has begun to have an impact and pay dividends? (see Chapter 13). Despite this of course, and as is also true for children's fitness, there is a clear 'polarization' of activity in children and therefore still a significant proportion of inactive youngsters.

The activity versus fitness debate

Given all of this, an important question we need to ask is whether the priority should be to 'get the buggers fit', to 'get them active', or both? For a number of years now researchers and practitioners alike have stressed the importance of focusing on and promoting physical activity rather than physical fitness, mainly for the reasons we have listed below. We revisit a number of these points and discuss them in more detail later in this book.

Reasons for focusing on and promoting physical activity in children include the following.

- There is no firm evidence to suggest that low levels of aerobic fitness are common among children and equivocal or contradictory evidence concerning whether children's fitness has declined over the years or not, yet there is evidence that a sizeable proportion of children are inactive and lead sedentary lifestyles.
- The idea that physical fitness is the ultimate goal is 'archaic' and is not supported by our current understanding of the links between fitness, activity and health in children. As Chapter 1 revealed, there is evidence that both fitness and activity are beneficial to health.
- Focusing too much on fitness may be counter-productive and could have as many negative consequences as positive ones. For example, many children may find it unpleasant, demeaning, and embarrassing and may be switched 'off' rather than 'on' to physical activity for life.
- The focus on fitness which was common practice for many years, has been unsuccessful in increasing physical activity levels. The evidence for this is that we have a largely inactive adult population. Some countries which had national fitness surveys for years have high proportions of inactive children and adults.
- In contrast to physical fitness, which is an attribute, increased physical activity is a behaviour and can therefore be accomplished by all children regardless of ability (or disability) or personal interests. It will also benefit those young people who need it most. Unlike physical fitness, physical activity is free from genetic and maturational influences (see Chapter 5) and it effectively 'levels the playing field', allowing all youngsters to participate and thereby succeed.
- A shift to promoting physical activity is more likely to be acceptable to the general public, including parents and students and particularly those who are sedentary or have low fitness levels.

In summary, both physical fitness and physical activity are desirable for children and promoting both should be beneficial (if approached in an appropriate way). However, for the reasons we have outlined and if resources and/or time are limited, which they inevitably tend to be in schools these days, we feel that your attention and energy would be better spent trying to 'get the buggers active' rather than 'fit!' From this point onwards therefore, we refer to promoting physical activity and healthy, active lifestyles in children, rather than fitness. Of course if you are successful, it is likely, though not necessarily inevitable (as Chapter 5 explains), that your students' fitness will also improve.

References

Armstrong, N. (2004), 'Children are fit and active – fact or fiction?', *Health Education*, **104**(6), pp. 333–5.

Armstrong, N. and Fawkner, S. G. (2007), 'Aerobic fitness', in N. Armstrong (ed.), *Paediatric Exercise Physiology*, pp. 161–88.

Craig, R. and Mindell, J. (2007), *Health Survey 2006. Volume 2. Obesity and Other Risk Factors in Children*. The Information Centre.

Durnin, J. V. G. A. (1992), 'Physical activity levels past and present', in N. Norgan (ed.), *Physical Activity and Health*. Cambridge: Cambridge University Press, pp. 20–7.

Jobson, M. (2007), Taking Part: *The National Survey of Culture, Leisure and Sport. Headline Findings from the Child Survey*. London: Department for Culture, Media and Sport.

Joint Health Surveys Unit (1998), *Health Survey for England: The Health of Young People 1995–1997*. London: HMSO.

Malina, R. M. (2007), 'Physical fitness status of children and adolescents in the United States: status and secular change', in G. R. Tomkinson and T. S. Olds (eds), *Pediatric Fitness. Secular Trends and Geographic Variability*, pp. 67–90.

Sport England (2003), *Young People and Sport in England. Trends in Participation 1994–2002*. London: Sport England.

TNS Social Research (2007), *2006/07 School Sport Survey*. London: TNS UK Limited.

Tomkinson, G. R. and Olds, T. S (2007), 'Secular changes in pediatric aerobic fitness test performance: The global picture', in G. R. Tomkinson and T. S. Olds (eds), *Pediatric Fitness. Secular Trends and Geographic Variability*, pp. 67–90.

Welsman, J. and Armstrong, N. (2000), 'Physical activity patterns in secondary school children', *European Physical Education Review*, **5**(2), pp. 147–57.

Appendix
Children's fitness, activity and health – true and false answers

Statement	T or F?
The onset of cardiovascular disease begins in childhood.	**T** – Even though the clinical symptoms of CVD do not become evident until much later in life, it is now recognized that CVD is partly a paediatric problem.
There is overwhelmingly strong evidence that physical activity is beneficial to children's health.	**F** – There is some evidence that activity during childhood is beneficial to health but strong evidence has yet to be provided. However, due to limitations in research, relationships may exist which have not yet been detected. In other words, the absence of evidence may not indicate evidence of absence!
Physical activity has been found to benefit chronic disease risk factors, body fatness, skeletal health and psychological well-being in young people.	**T** – More active children have generally been found to have healthier cardiovascular profiles, better mental health and to be leaner and have higher peak bone mass than their less active counterparts.
Childhood overweight and obesity is neither increasing nor decreasing in the UK.	**F** – Childhood overweight and obesity have increased in both sexes in recent years, and three in ten children are now classed as overweight or obese. Some experts have estimated that these figures will continue to rise and that two thirds of children will be overweight or obese by 2050.
Children's aerobic fitness generally increases with age.	**T** – Children's aerobic fitness shows a progressive, almost linear increase with age, although some studies show that from about 14 years, girls' aerobic fitness levels off.
Some children are very active whereas others are very inactive.	**T** – A number of studies have reported children's activity levels to range from very high to very low, with some youngsters being very active and others very inactive.
There is a good deal of evidence that children today are less fit than in the past.	**F** – There is relatively limited evidence on this issue and opinion seems to be divided. Based on an analysis of data over almost six decades, Armstrong and colleagues at Exeter University concluded that the aerobic fitness

Statement	T or F?
	of young people has not changed over the last 50 years, while data from performance tests has consistently indicated a decrease in aerobic fitness. This could, however, be a reflection of the rise in children's body mass over time rather than a true reduction in aerobic fitness.
Low aerobic fitness is common among children.	**F** – There is no firm evidence to suggest that low levels of aerobic fitness are common among children. Analysis of data collected at Exeter University over a 15-year period (on over 3,000 young people) has revealed that only 2 per cent could be classified as at risk due to a low level of aerobic fitness and a summary of the available field test data on children's fitness found that the majority of children meet or exceed criterion-referenced standards.
A sizeable proportion of children in the UK are inactive and lead sedentary lifestyles.	**T** – UK surveys reveal that a significant proportion of young people do not participate in physical activity and the most recent Health Survey for England reveals that a sizeable number fail to meet physical activity recommendations for young people.
Girls are more active than boys.	**F** – Research consistently shows boys to be more active than girls.
Physical activity levels increase with age, with the teenage years being the most active time.	**F** – Physical activity decreases with age and the teenage years appear to be the time of greatest decline.
People who are active during their childhood are more likely to be active in adulthood.	**T** – There is some evidence, albeit limited, that suggests that childhood activity influences adult participation. It is more likely that an active child will become an active adult.
Children are generally the fittest and most active group of the population.	**T** – Generally children are fitter and more active than adults and older adults. Fitness and activity levels decrease with age.
Most boys and girls are not fit enough to benefit their health.	**F** – There is no evidence to suggest that this is the case (see above).

II | How? – Understanding Children

3 | What switches children on and off?

Introduction

In Chapter 2 we revealed that:

Three in ten boys and four in ten girls fail to meet physical activity recommendations for young people, (meaning) that a sizeable proportion of children are inactive and lead sedentary lifestyles;

and

'Polarization' of activity (where there are extreme groups of very active and very inactive individuals), appears to be common in children.

This begs the question, why is it that some children, including some of your students, are active and switched on to physical activity and others are not? To answer this, you need to understand your students, the factors that influence their participation (or not) in physical activity, and the barriers they face to participation. Only in this way are you likely to be successful in your efforts to promote and influence their physical activity. Here we provide a summary of such factors and barriers, and consider the implications of this information to your practice. To inform your practice and approaches further, we also take a brief look at some of the characteristics of young people generally.

What switches children on and off physical activity?

There are a whole range of factors that are believed to influence people's physical activity. These are often called 'determinants' or 'correlates' of physical activity. These terms refer to the reproducible associations between a behaviour (in this case physical activity) and some factor. Knowing and understanding these determinants or correlates can help you to identify specific target groups to work with, as well as factors to try to change. For example, you might identify girls or underachievers as target groups, or factors such as attitudes or the physical education curriculum to change. In this way, you are likely to be more successful in influencing physical activity behaviour.

Although we still need to know much more about the correlates of physical activity in children, a number of consistent ones have been identified which can be classified into:

◆   Personal factors;
◆   Behavioural factors;
◆   Social and cultural factors;
◆   Environmental factors.

Based on these broad categories, we have summarized and presented a list of correlates of children's physical activity in Table 3.1. The list has been drawn and adapted from a comprehensive review by Sallis and others (Sallis et al., 2000) of correlates of physical activity in young people covering papers published over a 28-year period.

Table 3.1 The correlates of children's physical activity (PA)

	Factors		
Personal	*Behavioural*	*Social and cultural*	*Environmental*
Demographic and biological factors	Cigarette use	Parent PA	Access to facilities/programmes
Age	Alcohol use	Parent PA participation with youth	Parent provides transportation to PA
Ethnicity	Healthy diet	Parent benefits of PA	Season (summer/spring)
Sex (male)	Caloric intake	Parent barriers to PA	Milieu (rural)
Socio-economic status	Previous PA	Parental encouragement, persuasion	Neighbourhood safety
Single parent status	Sedentary time	Parent transports child	Time spent outdoors
Body mass index	Sedentary after school	Parent pays PA fees	Equipment/supplies available
Parent overweight/obesity	Sedentary on weekend	Subjective norms	Opportunities to exercise

Personal	Behavioural	Social and cultural	Environmental
Psychological/ cognitive factors	Sensation seeking	Peer influence/modelling	Sports media influence
Self-esteem	Fighting	Sibling PA	
Perceived competence	Meal regularity	Direct parental help in PA	
Self-efficacy	Community sports	Teacher support or modelling	
Body image	In school sports teams	Support from significant others	
Attitudes		Support from peers	
Outcome expectations		Coach support/modelling	
Sweat attitudes			
After school activity attitudes			
Dislikes physical education			
PA intention			
PA preference			
Perceived benefits			
General barriers			
Achievement orientation			
Talks loudly			
Self-motivation			
Enjoy exercise			
Stress			
Depression			
Knowledge of exercise/health			

As can be seen from Table 3.1, numerous factors are thought to influence children's physical activity. Trying to take all of these into account would be virtually impossible. Thankfully, some factors are more important than others and it is to these we now turn and recommend that you focus your attention and efforts on.

Therefore, to simplify matters somewhat, we have identified and briefly described the key correlates of children's physical activity on the following pages.

Theories/models used to study correlates of physical activity

First though, there are a number of psychological models or theories that it is useful to be aware of when developing your understanding of children's physical activity. These theories focus on personal, psychological and social correlates of physical activity. The common ones are:

◆ the Theory of Reasoned Action/Theory of Planned Behaviour
◆ the Social Cognitive Theory
◆ the Competence Motivation Theory/Theory of Achievement Motivation and Goal Orientations

A basic understanding of the main theories and their key factors may help you to provide an explanation of how or why a particular correlate affects behaviour. No one theory however, is likely to fully explain the physical activity behaviour of your students.

1. The Theory of Reasoned Action and the Theory of Planned Behaviour

The Theory of Reasoned Action says that a person's intention to be active and their physical activity behaviour are predicted by two factors: (i) their attitude towards physical activity, and (ii) perceived social pressure, or the beliefs of others and the extent to which the person wishes to comply with others' beliefs. The Theory of Planned Behaviour is the same as the Theory of Reasoned Action but also includes the factor of perceived behavioural control to account for when physical activity is not under a person's total control.

In other words, the theories suggest that if a person has a positive attitude towards physical activity and wishes or feels the need to please others (e.g. in the case of a child, their friends, parents or teachers), he/she will choose to be active.

2. The Social Cognitive Theory

In this theory, self-efficacy, which refers to a person's beliefs about their ability to perform a particular behaviour (in this case physical activity), is one of the most important means of changing behaviour. A person's perceived self-efficacy, in other words how capable they feel doing physical activity, is thought to influence both their uptake and persistence of activity.

3. The Competence Motivation Theory and the Theory of Achievement Motivation and Goal Orientations

These theories both stress that perceived competence is a major factor influencing motivation. If a person feels physically competent, they are likely to be more interested in physical activity and show greater effort. In addition, there are two major achievement goals that involve different conceptions of competence. For some individuals, success is norm-referenced, which means that for them competence is experienced by performing better than others (ego or performance goals). For others, success is self-referenced, which means that they experience competence through personal improvement (task learning or mastery goals).

The theories and children
As we highlight in the following section, while none of these theories have been studied in detail with children, young people's intention, attitudes towards physical activity, self-efficacy, perceived competence and achievement orientation have nonetheless all been found to relate to their physical activity behaviour. Further, this relationship has been consistent for intention, achievement orientation and perceived competence. Also, the more task oriented or focused a child is, the more likely they are to have higher perceived competence and therefore take up and adhere to physical activity.

Correlates of physical activity in children

Personal factors
Males are more active than females and during adolescence there is a decrease in physical activity with age. Inconsistent findings have been found for age, ethnicity and body mass index, and no relationship has been found between physical activity and body weight/fatness or socio-economic status.

Few psychological factors and none of the psychological theories described earlier have been studied in detail with children. But, some of the components within these theories have received support. For example, in adolescents, the following factors have been found to be positively associated with physical activity:

◆ achievement orientation;
◆ perceived competence;

◆   intention to be active.

Depression has been found to be negatively associated with physical activity. Put simply, more active individuals are less likely to suffer from depression.

Other factors that have been found to be related to physical activity, but inconsistently include:

◆   self-efficacy;
◆   body image;
◆   attitudes/outcome expectations;
◆   liking of physical education;
◆   benefits of physical activity;
◆   knowledge of exercise/health.

Behavioural factors
Few studies have examined behavioural factors in children and, from these, only a small number of consistent positive associations between behaviours and physical activity have been found. These include:

◆   healthy diet;
◆   sensation seeking;
◆   previous physical activity;
◆   participation in community sports.

In adolescents, there is a negative relationship between physical activity and time spent in sedentary activities after school and at weekends.

Social factors
During adolescence, the following social factors have been found to be positively associated with physical activity:

◆   parental support;
◆   support from significant others;
◆   sibling physical activity.

Surprisingly, other social factors such as peer modelling and perceived peer support have not. However, apart from parental activity/modelling, social factors have not been widely studied or consistently measured. It is therefore probably too early to dismiss the importance of many of these factors.

Environmental factors

Even less attention has been paid to the influence of the physical environment on children's physical activity. Despite this, consistent associations have been reported between physical activity and the following factors:

◆ access to facilities and programmes;
◆ time spent outside;
◆ opportunities to exercise.

Having identified the most important factors for you, we should also mention that some factors are unmodifable (or not possible to change) (e.g. age, sex, socio-economic status), whereas others are modifiable (or possible to change) (e.g. self-efficacy, self-esteem, knowledge, attitudes, enjoyment). This is important to recognize. Efforts to promote physical activity should be based on the modifiable factors and should inform your approach and the content and nature of any intervention or initiative. For example, as self-efficacy is a correlate of children's physical activity, then an approach or intervention that aims to increase self-efficacy, if successful, should also result in an increase in physical activity. In the same way, as knowledge of exercise and health influences physical activity, then a programme that aims to develop knowledge and understanding of exercise and health, should, if successful, also lead to increased physical activity. This order is important – the primary focus should be on changing the correlate or factor that controls the behaviour (physical activity), and not the behaviour itself.

If modifiable factors inform your approach and the content and/or nature of any initiative, then of what use are unmodifiable factors? Unmodifiable factors such as age or sex remind us that young people are not a homogenous group and that different approaches and strategies are therefore needed for different groups. These factors should be used to select appropriate target groups for interventions or initiatives. Based on your knowledge of these factors as well as your students' physical activity and needs, you may decide to focus your efforts on a specific group or groups such as girls, underachievers or ethnic minority students. Equally, you may choose a particular year or Key Stage, such as Year 10 or Key Stage 4.

Children's sedentary behaviour

As we pointed out in Chapter 1, the pressures and opportunities for children to be inactive and lead sedentary lifestyles these days are immense. Labour-saving devices and gadgets abound, as do a whole host of attractive sedentary pursuits, including TV/DVD watching, playing computer games and surfing the net, which all compete for children's precious leisure time. And, it seems that sedentary activities are winning! As we noted in Chapter 2, many children now spend over half of their waking hours in front of televisions and computers. Interestingly, research has found that the amount of time children spend watching television and playing video games is not necessarily inversely related to their physical activity levels. Nonetheless, there is no doubt that the more time children spend in these sedentary activities, the less time they have available for physical activity.

Furthermore, reducing children's sedentary behaviour, without specifically trying to promote activity has been shown to increase physical activity levels. There may be some mileage therefore in targeting and encouraging your students to reduce the time they spend in sedentary activities.

Common barriers

A number of barriers or obstacles to participating in physical activity have been reported by children in various studies and surveys over the years, many of which are similar to those faced by adults. The main ones include:

◆ 'Just can't be bothered' – a general lethargy or lack of motivation, or a preference for other activities in general.
◆ 'Not the sporty type'/perceptions of physical activity – sports facilities/the environment is often perceived as intimidating or alien to many children.
◆ Lack of time – difficulties in combining school and other work commitments with household chores and other social activities.
◆ Lack of confidence/embarrassment – in the form of self-consciousness, embarrassment and fear of exposure in front of others.
◆ Physical effort and discomfort – associated with physical activity. Aspects children dislike include going outside in bad/cold weather, getting cold, wet, hot, sweaty, dirty, having to get changed, etc.

◆ Social/cultural pressures – especially for girls who learn from an early age that physical activity is valued more for males than it is for females.

◆ Lack of freedom – there has been a significant decline in children's (and especially girls') freedom to be independently active outside of the home over the years.

◆ Dislike of activities – many children consider the activities frequently offered to them unappealing and irrelevant.

◆ Attraction of sedentary activities – as already acknowledged, TV/DVD viewing and computer game playing leaves less time for physical activity.

◆ Nannying approaches – the health message associated with physical activity is perceived by some youngsters as just another instruction to be followed.

Characteristics of young people

As if the matter was not already complex enough, understanding children's physical activity is complicated further by the often dramatic psychological, physical and social developmental changes that occur in this age group. As a teacher, you are no doubt aware that children are in a stage of transition: psychologically, in terms of attitudes, opportunities and preferences; physically, in terms of height, weight and body size; and socially, in terms of peer and friendship groups. This is also all relevant to you in your efforts to promote activity to your students.

Other characteristics of children that we feel are relevant to your work, and some of which are linked to the changes described above, are that they often:

◆ have low financial resources;

◆ have little actual control over their lives;

◆ are self-conscious/lack confidence (e.g. regarding their body image, how they look);

◆ have a limited concentration span (i.e. they rarely sustain any activity for very long);

◆ have a tendency towards rebellion (e.g. against instructions, authority figures, anything that is said to be 'good' for them);

◆ show cynicism (e.g. about the importance of and/or validity of health messages);

- ◆ feel invincible (e.g. 'it won't happen to me' syndrome);
- ◆ have a preoccupation with their body image (especially adolescent girls);
- ◆ are strongly influenced by peers (e.g. not wishing to stand out in the crowd).

Implications

All of the preceding information has important implications for how you promote physical activity to your students. The more you understand your students, their physical activity behaviour and their decision making, the more effective you are likely to be in promoting physical activity and in developing and implementing appropriate approaches and physical activity initiatives.

In Table 3.2 we present some of the factors and information covered earlier. More importantly though, we consider their implications and some recommendations for your everyday practice. Following the advice in each case should enable you to influence or change the factor or issue, which in turn should influence or change physical activity.

Table 3.2 Issues and implications or recommendations

Issue	Implication/recommendation
1. Attitudes towards physical activity are related to children's physical activity.	Aim to enhance/foster positive attitudes by stressing the positive outcomes of physical activity and by making physical education as enjoyable and positive an experience as possible.
2. Self-efficacy and perceived physical competence are related to children's physical activity.	Aim to enhance your students' perceived physical competence by giving them the opportunity to experience success. Choose activities appropriate to students' competence levels and avoid exposing pupils to failure.
3. Achievement orientation – a task orientation (as opposed to ego) is related to children's physical activity.	Encourage students to be task oriented (i.e. to focus on self-improvement), by encouraging a mastery environment (i.e. one which concentrates on effort/trying one's best, completing/mastering tasks and personal improvement, and de-emphasizes social comparison (who is 'best'), competition and scores).

4. Parental support and sibling physical activity are related to children's physical activity participation.	When and where possible, aim to involve parents and the family (e.g. in events) and keep them informed of school initiatives and physical education activities (e.g. via newsletters; at parents' evenings).
5. Access to facilities influences children's physical activity participation.	Make facilities readily accessible to students at school (e.g. lunch times; break times; after school). Also, try to introduce students to physical activities that do not require specialized facilities and can be performed at home (e.g. dancing; aerobics; walking).
6. Children's perceptions of physical activity and the belief that they are not the sporty type are barriers to physical activity participation.	Explore definitions of physical activity, physical fitness, exercise and sport with students to better their understanding. Recognize and value all forms of physical activity equally, including dance, sport, exercise and lifetime activities.
7. Lack of confidence/embarrassment are barriers to children's physical activity participation.	Provide a safe and supportive environment for students which will build their confidence and reduce risk of embarrassment. Avoid tasks which are likely to cause embarrassment (e.g. whole-class demonstrations) or which involve unfair social comparison.
8. The physical effort and discomfort of physical activity are barriers to children's participation.	Provide a safe and supportive environment for students by allowing them to wear warm clothing if going out in bad weather, or if possible, use an indoor venue. Ease students into physical situations gradually. Match individuals on the basis of size, strength and ability and allow them to work at their own level.
9. Social/cultural pressures and expectations are barriers to children's participation (especially girls).	Challenge myths and stereotypes in the curriculum and in the opportunities provided to students in curricular and extracurricular time. Provide positive images and role models around school which boys and girls can relate to.
10. Many children dislike the activities often offered to them and find them irrelevant.	Offer students a broad range of activities that match their needs and interests. Provide them with the opportunity to develop skills, knowledge and understanding in activities they will be likely to pursue

	into adult life. Introduce new, novel activities (e.g. boxercise, aqua, Pilates, ultimate Frisbee, pop lacrosse).
11. Children have a tendency towards rebellion against instructions, authority and anything that is said to be good for them.	Aim to avoid being too directive or authoritative in your approach. Provide students with knowledge and experience of physical activity and empower them to make their own informed choices.
12. Children feel invincible and live in the present – 'it won't happen to me' syndrome.	Stress the short-term (e.g. feeling better; having more energy; improved muscle tone and fitness) as well as the long-term benefits (e.g. reduced risk of CHD) of physical activity.
13. Time children spend in sedentary activities restricts the time available for physical activity.	Discuss the advantages and disadvantages of sedentary pursuits with your students and raise their awareness that too much time spent in sedentary activities could be harmful. Encourage an 'everything in moderation' approach.

Reference

Sallis, J., Prochaska, J. and Taylor, W. (2000), 'A review of correlates of physical activity of children and adolescents', *Medicine and Science in Sports and Execise*, **32**, pp. 963–75.

4 | How often, how hard, how much?

Introduction

Now that we have established the benefits of physical activity (and fitness) to children (Chapter 1), children's physical activity (and fitness) levels (Chapter 2), and the factors that switch youngsters on or off physical activity (Chapter 3), an important question that remains is how much physical activity should children do? We aim to answer this question in this chapter by looking at the current physical activity recommendations for young people and their practical application. Alongside these, we also consider the government's target for physical education and school sport and the link between the physical activity recommendations and the government's target. Finally, we discuss the value of the physical activity recommendations as well as their limitations, some issues and cautions to be aware of in using and applying them to your students, and we also present some ideas for implementation.

'No gain without pain' – moderate versus vigorous physical activity

The saying 'no pain without gain' has been frequently quoted and practised by fitness instructors, sports coaches and physical education teachers over the years. Simply, the belief has been that exercise has to hurt to do any good and that we need to be pushed to our limits. Indeed, it is perhaps not surprising that this message also 'caught on' in physical education. Given the accepted responsibility schools and teachers have to promote healthy, active lifestyles, plus the growing concerns over children's physical activity, fitness and health, many physical education teachers may have felt under pressure to tackle these concerns 'head on'. Consequently, in their well-meaning efforts to get youngsters more healthy, active and fit through physical education, the 'no pain no gain' message may to some, have seemed sensible and wholly appropriate.

Whilst there might be truth in the 'no pain no gain' message for a minority of individuals, for example, high-level sports performers and aspiring gold medal winners who are prepared to push themselves to the limit in training and competition, it does not hold true and neither is it appropriate for the majority of the population. It is certainly not the message or experience you should be giving your students in physical education lessons. We will explain why.

The 'no pain no gain' message advocates a hard-line approach to exercise involving practices that are considered undesirable, misguided and inappropriate for children. These might include forced fitness regimes and fitness testing, 'hard' exercise such as arduous cross-country running, or dull, boring and repetitive drill-type activities. These practices we feel are not only guaranteed to turn most youngsters off rather than on to physical education, sport and physical activity, but they may be at the expense of developing their knowledge and understanding about physical activity and the physical and behavioural skills necessary for a physically active lifestyle. We revisit these issues in more detail in relation to the philosophy and delivery of health and fitness within the curriculum in Chapters 7 and 8. All we wish to note here is that in order to influence children's physical activity within school and physical education, their activity experiences must be positive, enjoyable, varied, meaningful and most of all pain*less*!

A 'no pain no gain' approach is also misguided for other reasons. Over the years there has been a shift in emphasis from 'hard training to improve fitness', towards 'enjoyable participation in activity for health'. While we know that training effects in both adults and children will occur through participation in high intensity exercise, what is less well known is that less intense and 'painless' exercise also has benefits. In other words, physical activity does not have to be strenuous and hurt for it to do us good. Research has shown that moderate levels of physical activity (equivalent in intensity to brisk walking) are beneficial for health and can reduce the risk of heart disease, obesity, and improve mental health. Also, because moderate intensity activity feels comfortable, it can be performed for longer. This is significant because it is the total amount of physical activity or energy expended (not the intensity) that is important for health and weight management. Moderate activity is also safer and less likely to lead to injury, and more achievable, appealing and enjoyable for children. Further, moderate activity is the recommended type of activity in current physical activity recommendations for young people which we discuss later in this chapter.

In our view, more accurate and alternative messages to give your students, and ones that are likely to be more attractive and acceptable to them, include:

◆ 'physical activity does not have hurt to do you good';
◆ 'no pain and there is gain';
◆ 'it doesn't have be hell to be healthy'.

We now turn attention to the amount of physical activity children should do.

Physical activity recommendations for young people

Early developments

Any attempts to promote physical activity in children should be based on formal and accepted physical activity recommendations. However, while for a long time there has been strong agreement on the amount and type of physical activity that adults should do to benefit their health, this has not always been the case for young people. In fact, for a number of years, the basis for the recommended amount of exercise young people should do was based on studies conducted on adults, and adult physical activity recommendations were applied to, or imposed on, children with no clear rationale. We are pleased to report that in the last ten years or so a good deal of progress has been made, and physical activity recommendations for young people have been developed based on the most up-to-date scientific evidence and expertise available.

Initially, recommendations for young people were formulated and published in the United States in the late 1970s and early 1980s. However, these early recommendations were broadly the same as for adults and their appropriateness was soon questioned. For example, in 1988 the American College of Sports Medicine proposed that children should engage in 20 to 30 minutes of vigorous exercise every day. Efforts have since been made to move away from 'adult'-like guidelines that focused on fitness, to recommendations that would promote physical activity goals and enhance future health and well-being. Therefore, recognizing the limitations of using adult guidelines with children, it was not long before further guidelines were developed for young people in the US. These included the 'Children's Lifetime Physical Activity Model' guidelines (Corbin et al., 1994) and 'Physical Activity Guidelines for Adolescents' (Sallis and Patrick, 1994). Overall though, the US recommendations have received little attention in the United Kingdom. A few years later, UK physical activity recommendations were developed for children.

Physical activity recommendations for young people in England

Recommendations for young people in England were developed by the Health Education Authority (HEA) in 1998. Their aim was to not only develop physical activity recommendations, but to produce a policy framework from a public health perspective that would maximize the opportunity for young people in England to participate in and benefit from a lifetime of regular, health-enhancing physical activity. Following a process of expert consultation and a review of the evidence surrounding physical activity and young people, the policy framework 'Young and Active?' was published in June 1998 (HEA, 1998). It provided an up-to-date review of the evidence available and guidelines on the recommended level and type of physical activity for young people aged 5 to 18 years. These recommendations have since been uniformly adopted and promoted.

The physical activity recommendations
The current recommendation is that:

All young people should participate in physical activity of at least moderate intensity for *one hour per day.*

Young people who currently do little activity should participate in physical activity of at least moderate intensity for *at least half an hour per day.*

A secondary recommendation is that:

At least twice a week, some of these activities should help to enhance and maintain muscular strength and flexibility and bone health.

The reasons for the one hour a day recommendation are that:

- most young people are currently doing 30 minutes of moderate physical activity per day on most days;
- childhood overweight and obesity is increasing;
- many young people possess at least one modifiable risk factor;
- many young people have symptoms of psychological distress.

The policy framework suggests that examples of moderate intensity activities may include brisk walking, cycling, swimming, most sports and dance:

- carried out as part of transportation, physical education, games, sport, recreation, work or structured exercise or for younger children as part of active play;
- performed in a continuous fashion or accumulated throughout the day.

The reasons for the secondary recommendation are that:

- participation in strength and weight-bearing activities is positively associated with bone mineral density and can be related to reduced risk of osteoporosis;
- muscular strength is required to perform activities of daily life (e.g. lifting, carrying, bending, twisting);
- trunk strength and muscular flexibility may be associated with reduced risk of back pain in later life.

Activities suggested to enhance strength include play, such as climbing, skipping or jumping, and structured exercise such as body conditioning or resistance exercises. Activities suggested to promote bone health include weight-bearing activities such as gymnastics, dance, aerobics, skipping, and sports such as basketball.

The government's target for physical activity

In 2002, government concerns about children's health and well-being led to a national strategy in England around physical education and school sport (referred to as the Physical Education School Sport and Club Links (PESSCL) Strategy but now known as the Physical Education and Sport Strategy for Young People (PESSYP) Strategy) (see Chapter 13 for further details). At the same time, the government set a national target (referred to as the Public Service Agreement target):

To ensure that 75 per cent of children do two hours of high quality physical education and school sport a week by 2006 and 85 per cent by 2008.

This is commonly referred to as the 'two hours a week' target. The government announced that the 75 per cent target had been met in 2006 and that the 85 per cent target for 2008 had already been achieved in 2007. There is also a long-term government ambition for 2010:

To ensure that all children should have two hours of curriculum physical education and the opportunity to access a further two to three hours of sport beyond the curriculum per week.

This is being referred to as the 'five hours a week' target.

The above is good news as it means that the government continues to explicitly support and value the role of physical education and school sport in contributing to young people's health and well-being. For example, the government is striving to reach its targets through the numerous programmes within the PESSYP strategy (see Chapter 13 for details). As a result, every school in England now belongs to a School Sport Partnership and the emergence of new specialized roles such as 'competition managers' has led to pupils being offered an increased and broader range of activity opportunities within and beyond the curriculum. The reference to 'high quality' physical education and school sport is also significant as it is important that children's experiences are successful, enjoyable, inclusive, relevant and developmentally appropriate.

The link between the physical activity recommendation and the government targets

The physical activity recommendation and government targets are different but they complement each other. The 'one hour a day' physical activity recommendation is how active children should be to gain health benefits. The most recent 'five hours a week' target is the amount of activity schools should be offering all children by 2010.

The 'one hour a day' recommendation adds up to seven hours of physical activity a week, while the government target adds up to five hours a week. Clearly, there is a mismatch here. Furthermore, the mismatch is probably even greater when one considers that children are not actively moving all of the time during physical education lessons and school sport sessions. For example, they may be changing, observing, analysing, coaching or officiating.

The assumption, therefore, is that children will find ways of being active for at least two to three hours away from the school setting such as in and around the home, with family, friends or individually.

The physical activity recommendation and government targets do, however, support each other in that the latter provides increased opportunities for children to achieve the 'one hour a day' recommendation. It is also hoped that the high-quality experiences in physical education and school sport will motivate and entice children to be active in their own time, and to pursue activities that they particularly enjoy.

Issues and recommendations for applying the recommendations in practice

Here we look at the physical activity recommendations in more detail, analyse their main strengths and limitations, and we propose some recommendations for applying them in practice.

Strengths

Appropriate – These are the first age and culturally appropriate recommendations to be developed. They are therefore welcomed and significant, and suggest that progress in the area is being made.

Promote a consistent message – The common message is that young people should aim to do one hour of moderate physical activity a day, which is in keeping with the latest adult recommendations which also promote participation in regular moderate physical activity. For the first time therefore, we have a consistent 'public health' message about physical activity.

Realistic and attainable – If physical activity recommendations are to be useful, they must be realistic and attainable by the group they are intended for. To ensure this, the recommendations have been informed by research on young people and physical activity. By emphasizing moderate rather than vigorous physical activity, they are likely to be more attainable and enjoyable for children. As we mentioned earlier, the message that physical activity does not have to be painful or strenuous for it to have benefits should make the prospect of participating more appealing to youngsters.

Also, the message that physical activity does not have to be continuous, but can be accumulated or built up over the course of the day, is likely to make the recommendations more appropriate and relevant, especially to younger children. As we explained in Chapter 2, children rarely sustain activity for very long – their activity tends to be sporadic and transitory. Previous guidelines that have recommended sustained physical activity (e.g. for 20 minutes or more) are not appropriate for many children.

Differentiated – Differentiated guidelines which allow for different targets to be set to cater for the needs of all children is another sensible feature of the HEA recommendations. Although the aim is for all young people to be active for one hour per day, those who currently do little activity are advised to aim for half an hour per day.

Physical activity versus exercise – We feel that it is also appropriate that the recommendations have adopted the term 'physical activity' rather than 'exercise'. Common perceptions of exercise are that it involves hard work, effort, strenuous activities, gyms and organized sports. As a result, it is often thought to be unattractive, irrelevant or even intimidating. Physical activity, on the other hand, which is a broad, all inclusive term that includes exercise, sport, play, dance and active living such as walking, housework and gardening, is undoubtedly more attractive and relevant.

Flexible – The recommendations are flexible. The aim is for young people to be active daily, but the recommendations acknowledge that physical activity can vary from day to day in type, setting, intensity, duration and amount, and that the methods of meeting the recommendations may also vary according to a child's stage of maturation. For example, many children are likely to achieve the one hour recommendation during play, whereas teenagers may be more likely to meet it through more structured activity.

Simple – Physical activity recommendations and messages can often seem complicated, overly technical and confusing. Yet, we argue that precise, accurate and scientific physical activity guidelines are useless if few want or are able to follow them. Compared with some previous guidelines, the recommendations are presented in relatively 'user' and 'child-friendly' language. In the past, complex guidelines relating to activity intensity in particular have been offered. For example, that activity intensity should be between a specific percentage of maximum heart rate (e.g. 60–90 per cent for fitness, 55–90 per cent for health).

Such concepts relating to intensity are difficult for children to grasp. The existing recommendations provide and define a clear 'intensity' message, recommending activities of at least moderate intensity.

Promotion of different fitness components – The recommendations promote a range of components of physical fitness, including muscular strength and endurance and flexibility, as well as aerobic fitness. Muscular strength and endurance and flexibility are often neglected components of fitness and this was the first time that these components were formally included within guidelines for children. Muscular strength and flexibility exercises can provide a number of benefits to children, including improved performance, posture, reduced risk of injury and protection against future back pain and osteoporosis. We believe that including a specific recommendation to promote these aspects represents sound, common-sense practice.

Limitations

Limited research evidence – The scientific evidence on which the physical activity recommendations are based is still relatively weak and there is still confusion and controversy over the amount of physical activity children need for health benefits. For this reason, some have suggested that guidelines should focus on aspects other than health, such as the establishment of activity habits. This would avoid the difficult question of how much activity is necessary and the temptation to adopt recommendations regardless of whether they are scientifically proven or not.

Frequency and time – We cannot assume that children will be able to make time, will wish to, or will find suitable opportunities to exercise so frequently (daily) and for as much time (one hour) as the primary recommendation suggests. The commonly held view that children have ample time and energy for activity is debatable, especially for older children with school, home and possibly part-time work commitments. As we highlighted in Chapter 3, time is a common barrier to being active for many children, just as it is for adults. The message from the recommendations, of course, is that activity may be performed continuously or accumulated throughout the day, but this still requires children to be motivated enough and to know how to make and build in enough time for this.

Recommendation – When encouraging your students to work towards the one-hour recommendation, help them to recognize the barriers which restrict their physical activity (such as a lack of time, money, facilities, transport), and find ways to overcome them. In addition, help them to appreciate the broad and full range of physical activity opportunities available to them, and time-effective ways of incorporating such activities into their daily lives (e.g. walking or cycling to school, the shops or to meet friends). This could be addressed within the physical education and/or personal, social and health education curriculum.

Misleading and flawed? – Due to the limited evidence available, neither the minimal (least) nor the optimal (most desirable) amount of physical activity for young people is known. Therefore, engaging in less activity than is recommended does not mean that it will not be beneficial. Every increase in physical activity can potentially have some health benefits for young people. A simple message to 'try to do a bit more' may lead to some of the same benefits and is likely to be easily achievable by most.

In addition, the rationale provided for one hour (as opposed to 30 minutes) of at least moderate activity on most days could be flawed. The argument given against a guideline for 30 minutes of at least moderate activity on most days of the week was that, although most young people are currently meeting this, childhood overweight and obesity is increasing and many young people have been found to have at least one modifiable coronary heart disease risk factor. While this is true, it is rather simplistic to blame lack of physical activity for such problems or conditions. The causes of all chronic diseases are multidimensional and complex and not yet fully understood.

Exposure – To be of any use, physical activity recommendations need to be widely disseminated and promoted so that they are comprehensible to all involved in promoting physical activity to children. At this point in time, there is little evidence to suggest that this has happened. Physical activity recommendations seem to have received little attention and had little impact. For example, as far as we can tell, and from our experiences of working with schools and teachers over a number of years, the recommendations do not seem to have reached a number of schools and therefore are rarely included within the formal curriculum.

Recommendation – We encourage you to 'spread the word' and disseminate and promote the physical activity recommendations and key messages to colleagues, other schools and to your students.

Confusion – It seems that some confusion has arisen in recent years between the physical activity recommendation of one hour per day and the government's target of two hours a week of high-quality physical education and school sport. As noted earlier however, whilst the two complement each other, they are different. It is important that the one hour a day physical activity recommendation is promoted as this relates to how active children should be to gain health benefits.

Recommendation – Make best use of the opportunities and time provided through the government target to support the one hour a day recommendation. Also, focus on achieving the 'highest quality' physical education and school sport experiences possible for your students to motivate and encourage them to be active in their own time.

Acceptance – An important question for us would seem to be how the recommendations, if they are promoted, are likely to be interpreted and accepted by children as well as parents, teachers and health professionals. Studies have generally shown limited awareness by people (including adults and young people) of physical activity guidelines. Further, a study conducted by the Health Education Authority a few years ago now involving 16- to 24-year-old young women revealed uncertainty and scepticism about the precision and validity of the messages and guidelines.

Recommendation – Discuss the nature, scope and use of physical activity recommendations with your students. In addition, share with them the cautions that are presented later in the chapter.

Safe implementation – Whilst the secondary recommendation for muscular strength and flexibility and bone health is a positive addition, we would stress that the recommendation should be interpreted carefully and implemented with caution. There are some specific safety considerations in carrying out strength and flexibility work with children and there are risks associated with some forms of strength and flexibility training. These are mainly associated with unsupervised lifting of heavy weights and with extreme stretch positions. The intention behind the recommendation is not to encourage children to perform 'adult-type' formal strength and flexibility exercises – rather that developmentally appropriate versions of these be taught to children and adolescents. We feel though, that more guidance could have been forthcoming in support of this secondary recommendation to avoid any misunderstandings or misinterpretations.

Based on a review of the relevant literature, a series of recommendations have been made which are reproduced for you in

Table 4.1. Further guidance on resistance exercise in young people has also been published by Stratton (2004a; 2004b) on behalf of the British Association of Sport and Exercise Sciences and by the Association for Physical Education (2008).

Recommendation – If recommending or incorporating structured strength and flexibility work with your students, be aware of and implement the recommendations relating to the amount and type they should be doing (see Table 4.1).

Table 4.1 Recommendations for strength and flexibility exercises with children

Recommendations

Weight or load-bearing activities are recommended for children of all ages. These include activities in which the body has to support (i) all or part of its own weight (e.g. running, jumping, dancing, gymnastics); (ii) the weight of additional objects (e.g. a throwing or striking implement such as a bat, ball, bean bag, quoit, hoop).

Young children (4–11 year olds) should be involved in a wide range of weight-bearing activities for both the upper body (e.g. climbing, throwing, catching, striking) and the lower body (e.g. running, jumping, hopping, skipping). **9 to 11 year olds** can additionally be involved in developmentally appropriate low level exercises involving their own body weight such as 'easy' curl ups (with legs bent and hands along floor) for the abdominal ('tummy') muscles and 'easy' push ups (against a wall or in a box position) for muscles in the arms and chest.

Education about **back care** is important for **all children**. Safe lifting, carrying and lowering involves:

◆ getting close to the object being lifted;
◆ keeping a wide solid base with feet apart and firmly on the ground;
◆ using the large leg muscles rather than the back muscles;
◆ tightening the abdominal muscles;
◆ keeping the back straight when lifting or lowering;
◆ holding the object close to the body;
◆ getting assistance if the object is very heavy.

Older children (11 years and upwards) should be involved in differentiated exercises involving their own body weight, particularly for muscles which assist good posture (i.e. the back and abdominal muscles). **It is recommended that young people learn how to perform body resistance exercises with good technique before progressing on to exercises involving external weights.**

Low resistance external weights (such as light dumb-bells, elastics and tubing) can be safely used by older children (11 year olds and upwards). **Medium to high resistance external weights** (as is possible with fixed equipment such as a multi-gym and with free weights such as dumb-bells and barbells) are only advisable with 14 to 18 year olds. Lifting **near-maximal weights** is only appropriate for young people aged 16 to 18 years who have reached the final stage of maturation.

Each **strength exercise** should be performed no more than ten times before resting the muscles involved. Unfamiliar exercises should be performed four to six times, progressing over time to ten repeats. **Controlled lifting and lowering** should be emphasized. There should be gradual progression from one to three sets. Each session should include exercises for a balanced range of major muscle groups. No more than three sessions a week of strength exercises is recommended and there should be at least one day's rest between sessions. Any increases in frequency, intensity or duration should be gradual (by only 5 to 10 per cent at a time).

Stretching exercises are recommended for all age groups, especially older children (11 years and upwards). Stretching should only be performed following cardiovascular activity when the muscles are warm. Each **stretch** should be moved into slowly and held still. The holding time for stretches should vary from 6 to 20 seconds (depending on the weather conditions, how warm the muscles are, and the age and maturity of the children). Young children (4 to 11 year olds) can learn simple and frequently-used stretches (e.g. whole-body stretches; calf stretches) while older children can learn stretches for specific muscle groups (e.g. triceps, hamstrings). **It is recommended that stretches are taught within warm ups and cool downs**. The knowledge, understanding and skills associated with stretching should be progressively taught over time.

With reference to both strength and stretching exercises, the emphasis with all age groups should be on **safety and quality**, not quantity, with particular attention paid to **progression** and **balance**. Young people should understand the purpose of exercises and be able to perform them with good technique and at a developmentally appropriate level (i.e. one which matches their stage of physical and psychological maturity). They should know how to make exercises easier or harder.

The **learning environment** should be positive and non-threatening and the focus should be on **personal improvement**, not comparison with others. The delivery should aim to involve young people in their own learning and promote a **responsible attitude** towards safe, health-enhancing exercise behaviour.

Properly designed strength and flexibility training programmes for children should be:

(i)   child-centred and individualized, including developmentally appropriate exercises which match the physical and psychological maturity of the young person;

(ii)   progressive with only gradual increases in frequency, intensity or duration being made at any one time;

(iii)   balanced (i.e. only one part of a total exercise programme; incorporating all the major muscle groups);

(iv)   competently taught and closely supervised by an appropriately qualified adult.

Adapted, with permission, from J. Harris, 2001, *Health-related Exercise in the National Curriculum: Key Stages 1 to 4* (Champaign, IL: Human Kinetics), pp. 14–15.

Cautions

We have already highlighted a number of limitations and issues concerning using and applying the physical activity recommendations with children. For this reason, we wish to caution and propose that recommendations:

◆   are not strict rules, rigid prescriptions or unyielding standards;

◆   represent principles, 'not theorems or laws';

◆   should be used with common sense and sensitivity;

◆   should be viewed not as a starting point for children, but as a goal for them to progress towards;

◆   should take into account children's health and activity histories, physical fitness levels, functional capacities, personal circumstances, goals and preferences/dislikes.

Also, we firmly advocate the following key messages and guidance:

◆   all physical activity, performed safely, provides health benefits;

◆   even very low level physical activity (e.g. leisurely walking) is beneficial;

◆   avoid imposing standards on children or forcing them to participate in a regime of physical activity;

◆   avoid dictating the same starting point and rate of progression for all.

Summary recommendation – We recommend that you adopt an

individualized, personalized and differentiated approach when giving physical activity guidance to your students. Respect and treat your students as individuals and help and encourage them to set personal, attainable, short-term goals and to engage in the types and amounts of physical activity which are appropriate for and appealing to them. There should be no hierarchy of activities in the promotion of physical activity and your students should learn to value all forms and types of physical activity.

Implementing and helping your students to achieve the recommendations

Finally, in an effort to address some of the key issues associated with the physical activity recommendations and to help children to ultimately achieve them, we propose a number of ideas for implementing them with your students (see Table 4.2). These ideas complement and reinforce the key messages and philosophy we are keen to promote throughout this book.

Table 4.2 Ideas for implementing the recommendations

Issue	Implementation Idea
Key concepts/foci	Ensure that the key concepts and main foci of planning, delivery and evaluation are health, participation and physical activity, and are holistic and inclusive.
	Provide a structured programme which teaches all young people about the benefits and risks of physical activity and inactivity and provides them with opportunities to experience and learn through a broad and varied range of activities.
Developmentally appropriate activity	Consider and incorporate into planning and delivery the appropriateness of particular activities for differing maturity levels (e.g. full push ups are inappropriate for young children (under 11 years) as well as for some older children).
	Ensure that suitable alternatives are offered (e.g. climbing; gymnastic activities; 'easier' versions of exercises).

Issue	Implementation Idea
Flexibility/differentiation	Provide choices within activities (e.g. of exercise type and level of intensity).
	Do not 'put down' young people who opt for less demanding versions of activities – be positive and encouraging.
	Focus feedback on personal progress and improvement, not on achievement in relation to others.
Environment	Ensure that the physical activity environment is appealing (clean, warm, inviting).
	Ensure the physical activity environment reflects an inclusive and holistic philosophy (e.g. posters portraying individuals of differing shapes, sizes, colours, abilities, disabilities, etc.; equipment which caters for a range of abilities).
Encouragement/rewards	Show interest in what physical activity young people do (in school and in their leisure time).
	Offer and provide rewards (e.g. praise, treat) for increases in physical activity (e.g. joining in or helping out with a club or community event, including organizing, coaching and officiating) and also reductions in physical inactivity (e.g. watching less TV; spending less time playing on the computer).
Respect	Listen to and aim to respond to comments (positive and negative) made by young people about physical activity, sport, physical education and the activities offered to them (including in school through the extended curriculum).
	Do not ignore persistent and important issues such as gender, unappealing activities, showering, kit (in school).
	Ask young people for their views, ideas and suggestions about current and future developments.

Source: Cale and Harris (2001). Reprinted with permission.

References

Association for Physical Education (2008), *Safe Practice in Physical Education*. Leeds: Coachwise.

Corbin, C. B., Pangrazi, R. P. and Welk, G.J. (1994), 'Toward an understanding of appropriate physical activity levels for youth'. *Physical Activity and Fitness Research Digest*, Series 1, Volume 8, pp. 1–7.

Harris, J. (2000), *Health-related Exercise in the National Curriculum. Key Stages 1 to 4*. Champaign, IL: Human Kinetics.

Health Education Authority (1998), *Young and Active? Policy Framework for Young People and Health-enhancing Physical Activity.* London: HEA.

Sallis, J. F. and Patrick, K. (1994), 'Physical activity guidelines for adolescents: Consensus statement'. *Pediatric Exercise Science*, **6**, pp. 302–14.

Stratton, G. (2004a), *BASES Guidelines for Resistance Exercise in Young People* (Leaflet). Leeds: Coachwise Solutions.

Stratton, G. (2004b), 'BASES position statement on guidelines for resistance exercise in young people', *Journal of Sports Sciences*, **22**, pp. 383–90.

5 | Establishing how fit children are

Introduction

Fitness testing has been carried out with children for a number of years and is now practised in most schools. But, its purpose, value and place in the curriculum have been and remain a topic of much debate. In this chapter we explore physical fitness testing in so far as it relates to promoting physical activity in children. To begin with, we consider the purposes for and main methods of monitoring fitness. We then consider some of the issues and limitations with tests and testing before offering some recommendations and appropriate fitness testing ideas for use with your students.

The purpose of monitoring physical fitness

Fitness testing children can potentially serve a number of purposes within school. Common purposes include:

- to evaluate fitness programmes;
- to motivate students;
- to identify students in need of improvement;
- to identify students with potential;
- to screen students;
- to diagnose fitness needs for individual exercise prescription and improvement;
- to promote physical activity, and goal setting, self-monitoring and self-testing skills;
- to promote learning and positive attitudes.

Methods of monitoring physical fitness

In Chapter 1 we defined physical fitness and explained that it comprises health-related and performance (skill)-related components. The health-related components of fitness include cardiovascular fitness, muscular strength and endurance, flexibility and body composition, and can be measured in the laboratory or field by a range of different fitness tests. It is the field-based tests of health-related fitness that are of interest to us here because these components are related to specific 'health' or disease outcomes and can easily be conducted in schools.

Field-based physical fitness tests

Physical fitness testing in the field or in school usually involves the administration of a battery of simple tests to evaluate different components of fitness. Below and in Table 5.1, we summarize some of the most commonly used tests.

Aerobic fitness/capacity – Distance runs have for a long time been the most commonly used field measures of aerobic fitness with children. The mile run/walk, in which children complete the distance as quickly as possible, has been included in several fitness test batteries. Other variations include the one and a half mile run, or the nine or 12 minute run for distance. The Multistage Fitness or 'bleep' test, which is a progressive shuttle run test for the prediction of maximum oxygen uptake is also popular (see References). Because it is a maximal test, however (i.e. it involves individuals exercising to the point of exhaustion), controversy surrounds its appropriateness for use with children.

Muscular strength and muscular endurance – Field tests of muscular fitness involve resisting or moving part or all of the body weight. The stomach and upper arm tend to be the areas most often tested and common exercises include sit ups or curl ups, pull ups and flexed arm hangs. The tests usually involve performing as many repetitions of the exercise as possible in a set time or before reaching exhaustion. An example of the latter is the 'progressive abdominal sit up test' which involves performing the curl up in time to a controlled and timed 'bleep' until the individual can no longer continue (see References).

Flexibility – Because poor flexibility in the lower back and hamstring region can be a cause of low back pain, common field tests of flexibility assess the range of motion at the hip joint. By far the most commonly employed test is the sit and reach. Others include the shoulder stretch or the arm lift.

Body composition – In the field, body composition is normally estimated using anthropometry (the measurement of body dimensions). The body mass index (BMI) has often been used, though the measurement of skinfold thicknesses is another common method that can provide a useful indicator of children's body fatness. Skinfolds are usually taken from a few selected sites of the body (e.g. the triceps, biceps, subscapular, suprailiac, the front thigh and medial calf in children). The sum of the skinfolds is then used as an indication of total body fat.

If using fitness tests with your students, you may choose to develop your own tests, test batteries and standards of performance to assess their physical fitness. Alternatively, you could use the test items and procedures we suggest later in this chapter or one of a growing number of commercial fitness test batteries. A number of formal fitness test batteries have been developed over the years, mainly in the United States, but also in Canada, Australia, Europe and elsewhere. The major batteries have a number of similarities. All measure common components of health-related fitness and many contain the same or similar tests.

Table 5.1 A summary of some of the more common field tests of physical fitness for children

Component	Measurement Procedures
Aerobic fitness/ capacity	Distance/timed walks/runs (1, 1.5 miles; 9, 12 minutes) Step tests Multistage Fitness test
Muscular strength/endurance	Sit ups/curl ups Progressive abdominal sit up (curl up) test Pull ups Modified pull ups Push ups
Flexibility	Sit and reach Shoulder stretch Arm lift
Body Composition	Body mass index (BMI) Skinfold thicknesses Girth measures

One well-established test battery you may find useful is FITNESS-GRAM which forms part of FITNESSGRAM/ACTIVITYGRAM, a national educational assessment, data management and reporting software program developed in the US (see References). FITNESS-GRAM is a comprehensive physical fitness assessment and reporting programme that includes a variety of health-related fitness tests and which uses criterion-referenced health standards to establish whether a student falls in the 'Healthy Fitness Zone' or 'Needs improvement'. The software provides individualized report cards that summarize the student's performance on each component of fitness and provides suggestions about how to promote and maintain good fitness.

A critique of field-based fitness tests and test batteries

If employing fitness testing with your students, it is important for both yourself and your students to be able to evaluate fitness tests and measuring procedures and to be aware of the pros and cons of tests. There a number of advantages and disadvantages which are common to all fitness tests and to fitness test batteries in general. For example, advantages include:

◆ tests are generally easy to administer and time efficient;
◆ tests are relatively safe and involve minimal equipment and cost;
◆ advances in the development and use of physical fitness tests for children have been impressive in recent years and a good deal of thought has now been given to the scientific evidence supporting a test;
◆ the emphasis of testing is now on the evaluation of health-related fitness components of fitness and has shifted in recent years from testing in isolation or for 'testing's sake', to an educational programme with testing as an integral part;
◆ many physical fitness programmes (e.g. FITNESSGRAM) are now packaged attractively and include test manuals, curricular guidelines and instructional materials to assist the user/teacher;
◆ some programmes have computerized feedback systems.

Disadvantages, measurement issues and concerns include:

◆ the appropriateness of some fitness tests for use with children is questionable (e.g. the Multistage Fitness test is a maximal test that has been developed for use with elite, adult populations);
◆ linked to the point above, children's responses to exercise

(metabolic, cardiopulmonary, thermoregulatory, perceptual) are different from adults – a special approach may therefore be required in administering tests to children;

◆ several of the popular field tests are still not based on sound physiological foundations;

◆ field tests generally provide only a crude measure of an individual's physical fitness;

◆ the reliability and validity of some fitness tests for use with children is questionable and there is a need for more evidence on the reliability and validity of tests and test batteries;

◆ many factors influence children's performance on fitness tests (and therefore the reliability and validity of the tests) and their fitness test scores. For example:
 – the environment/test conditions (temperature, humidity, wind speed/direction)
 – lifestyle (exercise/nutrition)
 – test procedures
 – motivation
 – intellectual and mechanical skill at taking the test
 – heredity or genetic potential
 – maturation

◆ the influence of these factors varies from test to test, and between testing sessions but heredity or genetic potential and maturation affect the test results the most;

◆ the debate over and limitations in using norm- and/or criterion-referenced standards, both of which have been frequently used in fitness test batteries with children (see Table 5.2).

In addition, of course, individual fitness test items have their own strengths and limitations, though we will leave you, with the help of your students, to work these out for yourselves.

Perhaps understandably, the many limitations we have pointed out regarding fitness tests with children have led to much scepticism concerning the value or meaning of test results. In particular, it is important to help your students to recognize the influence of genetics, heredity, maturation and motivation on test scores. For instance, it has been claimed that fitness tests simply determine the obvious, at best only distinguishing the mature and/or motivated from the immature and/or unmotivated. We could also add that fitness tests distinguish between those 'blessed' with 'fit' genes at birth, and those not.

Table 5.2 A summary of the advantages and disadvantages of norm- and criterion-referenced standards

Normative Standards		Criterion-Referenced Standards	
Involve the comparison of an individual's score with that of a reference group.		Absolute standards that specify the minimum levels of fitness thought to be required for health and to perform daily tasks.	
Advantages	Disadvantages	Advantages	Disadvantages
Allow quick and simple comparisons to be made with other students of the same sex and age.	Do not indicate desired levels of physical fitness.	Categorize individuals into groups that either meet or exceed minimum standards and those who do not.	Do not provide an incentive to students to achieve higher fitness levels.
	Do not provide any diagnostic feedback.	Attractive from a theoretical standpoint – they suggest there is a level of fitness (below that needed to be a successful athlete) that is satisfactory for health.	There is no evidence on the validity of the standards with young people – how standards have been determined and how carefully is not clear.
	Imply that 'more is better'.		There are sometimes large variations in standards developed for the same test items from one youth fitness test to another.
	Promote ego orientation.		Use of the standards (if not valid/accurate) could lead to misclassifications of fitness, which could have negative consequences for students.

Advantages	Disadvantages	Advantages	Disadvantages
	By failing to take maturation into account, they confuse the issue of relative fitness.		

To test or not to test? – issues

Apart from the limitations we have just identified, other concerns and issues have been aired concerning fitness testing children. You may therefore be wondering or asking yourself, why bother fitness testing? We should not, however, forget or overlook the purposes of testing children that we identified earlier. Fitness tests potentially have value and they can provide useful information on children's capabilities in a range of components of physical fitness. Alongside this though, you should also be aware of the following issues.

Fitness testing paradoxes

There are a number of fitness testing paradoxes which, as explained below, raise questions over the merits of testing.

- Fitness tests claim to assess health-related physical fitness yet do not provide any clinical measures of health status (e.g. blood pressure, blood lipids).
- Fitness tests emphasize safe healthy practice, yet some involve children performing tests which violate healthy behaviour and even, we feel, sometimes common sense. Batteries may claim to encourage good fitness behaviours, but the tests themselves may not always promote or involve this behaviour. For example, exercising to exhaustion as is required in the Multistage Fitness test, or performing as many sit ups as possible in one minute is not recommended practice.
- Fitness tests deprecate performance as a component of health-related fitness, yet in most test items performance is used as the basis for assessing fitness.
- The implications of children's fitness test results for health are still not well established or understood. As we noted in Chapter 1, there is evidence from scientific studies that children's fitness is

related to health. However, we do not know whether children who perform well or better on standard fitness tests are likely to be more healthy or healthier in the future.

Misunderstandings

It is often thought that fitness in children is primarily a reflection of the amount of activity they do, and that those who score high on fitness tests are active and those who do not are inactive. This assumption is inaccurate. The relationship between physical fitness and physical activity is low among children and a child's activity level cannot be judged from his or her fitness level. Physical activity is an important factor in developing fitness in adults, but for children, other factors such as those we highlighted earlier (e.g. maturation, genetics/heredity) are of equal or greater importance.

You could encounter problems if you try to link your students' fitness test scores to their activity levels. On the one hand, an active student who scores badly on a test may become disappointed, disillusioned, demotivated and switched off activity because he/she feels it does not pay off. Equally, an inactive student who scores well may be delighted with the result, conclude that everything is fine when it is not, and consequently, despite your efforts, may not be motivated to change. We discuss the potential influence of fitness tests on children and their activity levels further below.

Impact on children and children's physical activity levels

An important consideration for you is how fitness testing might affect your students socially and emotionally, and how it might influence their attitudes towards activity. As we highlighted in Chapter 3, these factors in turn are likely to influence their participation. Concern has frequently been expressed that fitness testing may in fact be counterproductive to the promotion of active lifestyles and may switch many youngsters off rather than on to activity. Fitness tests can be demeaning, embarrassing and uncomfortable for some children – often for those about whom there is most concern, such as the least fit, active or overweight.

The above is likely to be the case if fitness tests are misused or conducted improperly or insensitively. Also, be aware that tests may communicate a false message to children – that competition and excellence are necessary for health and fitness, which may further hinder your efforts to promote physical activity.

Supporters of physical fitness testing argue that testing motivates children to maintain or enhance their physical fitness or physical activity levels, increases knowledge, and promotes physical activity by fostering positive attitudes. In fact, little is known about whether fitness testing motivates children, or about children's knowledge and attitudes towards fitness tests. In parallel areas of education, evidence suggests that tests only motivate those students who do well. In terms of knowledge and attitudes, a study we came across that investigated what children 'thought, felt and knew about' the mile-run test found that children generally had little or no understanding of why they were being asked to complete the test and many disliked taking it, viewing it as a painful, negative experience to be dodged if at all possible!

An overemphasis on fitness

There is also concern that the administration of fitness tests could lead to too much attention on the products of 'fitness' and 'performance' rather than on the processes of 'health' and 'physical activity' behaviour. Certainly there is and has been an overemphasis on fitness by the media in recent years, with frequent calls to 'get children fitter'. However, from a public health and physical activity promotion point of view, we argue that the goal should be to influence the 'process', i.e. physical activity, rather than the 'product' of fitness. In Chapter 2, in the 'activity versus fitness' debate, we explained a number of good reasons why the promotion of physical activity rather than physical fitness is favoured.

Implementation of fitness tests

There have been a number of complaints over the way in which fitness tests are often implemented and conducted within the physical education curriculum. For example, testing can often be an almost irrelevant adjunct to the curriculum, or else dominate, and in some cases even constitute the entire fitness education programme.

We question curriculum time being spent on fitness testing if it (i) fails to positively influence students' activity levels or their attitudes towards physical activity, (ii) detracts from promoting the process of being active, and (iii) is at the expense of time being spent on more useful activity promoting activities, and of developing students' knowledge and understanding about physical fitness and what physical fitness tests measure. In our view, administering fitness tests simply to obtain fitness test data, without paying attention to its educational role is poor practice and quite frankly a waste of time.

Misuse of fitness test scores

Finally, be aware of the inappropriate or undesirable use of fitness test scores with children. Examples within the curriculum include test scores being used to grade students as the primary indicator of their achievement, to evaluate teacher competence, or as a measure of the success of a school or fitness programme. Using fitness tests for these purposes could have a number of undesirable consequences such as loss of interest in physical education and physical activity, a 'teaching to the test' mentality, students and teachers cheating on fitness tests, or the undermining of the confidence of some students who may find that, even with effort, they cannot achieve the fitness needed to get good grades or to meet teacher expectations. Some of these may seem extreme and a sorry state of affairs but beware, we have heard of such practices happening!

Fitness testing recommendations

If or when fitness testing you do not pay careful attention to the above issues and concerns, to how you approach and administer tests to your students, as well as to the methodological problems with testing we highlighted earlier, the answer to the question 'to test or not to test' would have to be 'not'! Physical fitness testing can be counter-productive to physical activity promotion and not be good use of time. As we have explained, fitness testing can be unpleasant and embarrassing for some children, and scores can be inaccurate and therefore misleading, unfair, and demotivating. For these reasons, you may decide to abandon fitness tests in favour of alternative methods of assessing children, such as monitoring their physical activity or knowledge, understanding, and attitudes towards physical activity. We look at some ways of doing this in the next chapter.

However, if fitness testing is carried out appropriately and in a meaningful way, and provided the factors and issues raised here are taken into account, then there is no reason why you should not test your students, and why testing should not play a valuable role in the promotion of physical activity and in educating your students about their physical activity and physical fitness. Prior to embarking on fitness testing though, we advise you to give careful consideration to the students in your class, how they are likely to respond to and cope with fitness testing, which tests are likely to be appropriate and inappropriate for them, and how the tests would best be conducted.

In a position statement in 1988, the Physical Education Association (PEA) – a former professional association for physical education teachers in the United Kingdom, since replaced by the Association for Physical Education (AfPE) – claimed that fitness testing and monitoring can be valuable components of a health-related fitness programme if they are used to: encourage positive attitudes towards health-related fitness; increase understanding of the principles underlying health-related fitness; and promote a lifetime commitment to health-related fitness.

We echo the PEA's sentiments but believe that to achieve this teachers need clear and consistent guidance on the use of fitness testing with children. Recommendations on fitness testing with young people have been made by a number of researchers and professional organizations in the US and the UK over the years. We have analysed, summarized and attempted to interpret and develop the key recommendations and messages for you in Table 5.3. If you follow these recommendations then your students are likely to benefit from their involvement in and experience of fitness testing.

Table 5.3 Recommendations for fitness testing with children

General
Fitness testing should be used to encourage and help students acquire and maintain fitness levels that are appropriate for their personal needs. It should be recognized that the majority of children are sufficiently 'fit' and that 'high level' fitness is not necessary for all children.
Fitness testing should not dominate or be an adjunct to a programme. Testing should be fully and appropriately integrated.

Content
Fitness testing should focus on the health-related components of fitness and primarily on the monitoring of those components which involve children engaging in physical activity (i.e. cardiovascular fitness, flexibility, muscular strength and endurance). Body composition should be addressed and, if dealt with sensitively, could be included as a measure, but as a static test it is less useful/desirable in terms of promoting/facilitating physical activity.
Fitness test batteries should include developmentally appropriate tests

(e.g. providing different versions of exercises). Tests designed for adults should be avoided, or modified, and sub-maximal tests selected.

It should not be assumed that fitness testing will increase students' activity levels. Ideally, the development and maintenance of lifelong activity habits should be addressed (i.e. the process), as well as fitness (the product), and activity promotion measures included (e.g. monitoring activity; raising awareness and providing access to activity opportunities; goal setting; self-monitoring and self-evaluation) alongside testing (some of these elements feature in FITNESSGRAM).

Organization/delivery

Testing should be student-centred and accessible to all students. Personal improvement over time should be the focus, not comparisons with others.

Fitness testing should be a positive and meaningful experience, presented in an individualized manner that provides students with personalized baseline scores and feedback from which to improve their activity and fitness levels. Testing should never be administered at the expense of lowering an individual's self-concept or confidence. The public nature of testing should be minimized and prior practice given on tests to help make children feel comfortable, at ease and to allow them to perform their best. Careful consideration should be given as to whether it is desirable and/or necessary to measure body composition, but if it is, this should be done as sensitively and privately as possible. Compulsory use of exhausting maximal tests should be avoided. It may be appropriate to incorporate fitness testing as a choice activity.

Fitness testing should promote learning, and health-related learning concepts should be delivered during the fitness testing process (e.g. explaining the relevance of each component and ensuring that students understand how to improve each component).

Fitness testing should adhere to and be consistent with good practice (e.g. it should include a warm up and cool down, safe exercise practices, familiarization with the testing procedures, and be conducted in a safe environment (i.e. well-ventilated, adequate space, with appropriate equipment).

Fitness testing should be made as much fun, as varied and as relevant as possible, and move beyond 'traditional' administration methods. For example, student choices, testing options, home tasks, self- and partner/peer (versus whole-group) assessments, encouragement of self-responsibility and goal setting, and the use of fun equipment may have much merit and be more developmentally appropriate and relevant ways of testing students' fitness.

Feedback/evaluation

Fitness test results should be communicated and used with students in a meaningful way that promotes affective and cognitive learning about maintaining and/or improving personal fitness. Fitness test scores should be interpreted and explained carefully, with recognition of their limitations.

Any standards employed in interpreting scores should be explained and should be criterion-referenced rather than normative standards. Criterion-referenced standards are achievable by the majority of students and reinforce the fitness–health link and the notion that one can be fit without being an elite athlete.

Whilst all students should be provided with feedback, it is particularly important that individuals identified as 'very low fit' are provided with appropriate and sensitive remedial support, encouragement and progress monitoring. This might involve suggestions for activities/exercises they can undertake in their leisure time, at home or in the local community, communication with parents, or in extreme circumstances, referral to their GP.

Test re-test procedures (e.g. administering a test at the beginning and again at the end of a unit of work, school year) should be implemented with caution and only if the intervening programme/unit was designed to produce change and promote fitness. Even then, programmes/units are often too short (6–8 weeks) to expect any measurable changes and testing could have a demotivating effect. The practice can also be time consuming and detract from learning time.

The use of external rewards or award schemes can be a useful tool for motivating students but should be used sparingly. They should not be used to bribe students or to reward performance. If employed, they should reward and encourage activity objectives (not fitness performance) and should be achievable by all.

Home influences on students' activity and fitness levels should be recognized in feedback/evaluation and parents/carers should be encouraged to show interest in their children's physical activity and physical fitness and to be positive role models

Source: adapted and developed from Cale, L. and Harris, J., *Exercise and Young People. Issues, Implications and Initiatives*, 2005, Basingstoke: Palgrave Macmillan. Reproduced with permission of Palgrave Macmillan.

Fitness testing ideas

Finally, if you do wish to use fitness testing with your students and do not have access to or wish to use a commercially available fitness test battery, then we have selected the following tests and testing methods you may like to try. These are practical, appropriate and sensible, and adhere to the recommendations shown in Table 5.3. We also include some supporting information which you can share with your students.

Description

The fitness tests measure three key health-related components of physical fitness. These components have been chosen as the priority here because they are important for the health of every young person, and the tests associated with each involve engagement in health-promoting physical activity.

◆ Aerobic fitness
◆ Muscular strength and endurance
◆ Flexibility

The major health conditions associated with low levels of each component are summarized below.

Health-related component of fitness	Associated health conditions
Aerobic fitness	Coronary heart disease; obesity
Muscular strength and endurance	Osteoporosis (fragile bones); back pain; poor posture
Flexibility	Back pain; limited range of movement; poor posture

That is not to say however, that you should not introduce your students to all components of health-related fitness, which also includes body composition (i.e. the proportion of body weight that is fat in contrast to lean body mass (muscles, organs, bones)). Indeed, students need to be aware of how important healthy body composition is and that it is associated with a reduced risk of obesity and joint problems (see Chapter 9 for further information).

With the support of the worksheets in the Appendix to this chapter, we recommend that students complete the following fitness tests and record and reflect on their scores at regular intervals (e.g. once a year). A choice of aerobic fitness tests are included, and some of the tests include differentiated options to cater for students' differing shapes, sizes and stages of maturation and development in any one class.

In carrying out the tests and recording the results, comparisons of students' performance should be made with their previous performances and with the 'Healthy Fitness Ranges' (criterion-referenced standards) (see Appendix). These should provide realistic and meaningful targets to motivate every student to improve. Students should then complete the self-review 'Thinking about your Fitness' questions, and be encouraged and supported in their actions to increase their fitness levels.

Safety considerations

Prior to testing, make sure that you are aware of any potential health problems of your students. Students who are unwell or injured should not undergo fitness tests. Advise any child who feels dizzy or faint during any of the fitness tests to stop immediately.

It is possible that a student could have a non-diagnosed congenital heart condition that may require special consideration or urgent attention during the administration of an aerobic fitness test. Sub-maximal aerobic fitness tests should reduce the risk of any such event occurring.

For each fitness test, guidance is given as to how the students should prepare for and recover from the test. We recommend that you follow this guidance carefully to minimize the chances of any problems arising during or after the tests.

Aerobic fitness

Aerobic fitness refers to the ability of the cardio-respiratory system (heart, blood vessels and lungs) to function efficiently and to cope with the demands made upon it. Good aerobic fitness is important for health as it is associated with a reduced risk of high blood pressure, coronary heart disease, obesity and some forms of cancer in adults.

Mini bleep test

This test is a shortened version of the Multistage Fitness or 'bleep' test. The bleep test is a maximal test and, as such, requires individuals to run to the point of exhaustion. Consequently, this test is not considered to be appropriate for all students within curriculum time. It may, however, be considered useful as an optional test for motivated, elite youngsters.

The short bleep test is a sub-maximal multistage test which provides an indication of aerobic fitness. It requires students to undergo a progressive 20-metre shuttle run to a set level and to record their heart rate immediately afterwards.

Resources
CD player
Multistage Fitness test CD (see References)
A flat, non-slippery surface permitting a continuous run of 20 metres
Measuring tape
Marker cones
'How fit are you?' record sheet

Preparation for test
A warm up is not required for this test as it is progressive, being easier at the beginning and gradually becoming more demanding. In this sense, there is a warm up built into the design of the test.

Students should wear shoes with non-slip soles and their shoelaces should be firmly tied. The 20-metre course needs to be measured and marked prior to the test. It is advisable that students listen to several minutes of the tape so that they are familiar with the instructions and sounds. It would also be helpful for them to have practised running to the CD so that they know that the beginning speed is very slow and it gradually increases in pace. Students should also be familiar with finding their pulse and recording their heart rate. If you have access to some heart-rate monitors these could assist this process.

The test can be performed in pairs, with one student performing the test and their partner observing technique and recording the heart rate score.

Test procedure
The students stand behind the start line at one end of the running area. They run across the 20-metre distance (which counts as one lap) and touch the line at the other end of the running area with their foot by the time the bleep sounds. At the sound of the bleep, they turn around and run back to the other end. Students should aim to arrive at the lines just before, or on the sound of, the bleep. If they arrive at the line before the bleep, they must wait for the bleep before starting the return journey.

A single bleep sounds at the end of each lap and a triple bleep sounds at the end of each minute. The triple bleep alerts the students that the pace will increase slightly.

The students stop at a particular level specified by yourself as the teacher. Recommended levels for different ages are shown overleaf.

However, if you know your students' capabilities well, you may wish to make a professional judgement about the suitability of these recommendations for particular groups of students and individuals.

Age	Girls	Boys
11	Level 3	Level 4
12–13	Level 4	Level 5
14–18	Level 4	Level 6

Immediately after stopping at the specified level, students locate their pulse and count it for 15 seconds. You should inform the students when to start and stop counting. The pulse count should be recorded on the 'How fit are you?' record sheet.

Recovery from test
Following this test, students should perform a cool down by gently jogging or walking for one to two minutes and then performing stretches for the calf (back of lower leg), hamstring (back of upper leg) and quadriceps (front of upper leg) muscles. Each stretch should be held still for 10 to 20 seconds.

Step test
This test requires students to step up and down on and off a bench for a set period of time and to record their heart rate immediately afterwards. This also provides an indication of aerobic fitness.

Resources
CD player and music with a steady beat of 120 beats per minute (or a metronome)
Standard gym benches
'How fit are you?' record sheet

Preparation for test
Prior to the test, students can perform some hip, knee and ankle mobility exercises for a few minutes. Examples include heel–toe actions, heel raises, knee lifts, knee bends and hip circles.

Students should wear shoes with non-slip soles and their shoelaces should be firmly tied. It is advisable for students to have practised stepping on and off a bench to the music so that they are familiar with the pace required. Students should also be familiar with finding their pulse and recording their heart rate. If you have access to some heart-rate monitors, these could assist this process.

The test can be performed in pairs, with one student performing the test and their partner observing technique and recording the heart rate score.

Test procedure
The students stand behind a standard gym bench (with no more than six to any one bench). On a signal from you, they step up onto the bench and down in time with the music. The rhythm is 'up, up, down, down'. The students should ensure that their heels are placed on the bench when they step onto it. The students stop after a certain length of time, as specified by you. Recommended test durations are presented below. However, if you know your students' capabilities well, you may wish to make a professional judgement about the suitability of these recommendations for particular groups of students and individuals.

Age	Girls	Boys
11	3 minutes	4 minutes
12–18	4 minutes	5 minutes

Immediately after stopping, students sit down on the bench, locate their pulse and count it for 15 seconds. You should inform the students when to start and stop counting. The pulse count should be recorded on the 'How fit are you?' record sheet.

Recovery from test
Following this test, students should perform a cool down by gently jogging or walking for one to two minutes and then performing stretches for the calf (back of lower leg), hamstring (back of upper leg) and quadriceps (front of upper leg) muscles. Each stretch should be held still for 10 to 20 seconds.

Muscular strength and endurance

Muscular strength and endurance refer to the ability of the musculo-skeletal system (bones, muscles, joints, tendons, ligaments) to work against a resistance over a period of time. Good muscular strength and endurance is important for health as it is associated with a reduced risk of osteoporosis, poor posture, back pain and restrictions in movement.

Curl up

The curl up test measures the muscular strength and endurance of the straight abdominal muscle (rectus abdominis). Two versions of curl ups are described, an easier version (curl up A) and a more demanding version (curl up B).

Resources
Mat
CD player and music with a steady beat (about 120 bpm) (optional)
'How fit are you?' record sheet

Preparation for test
Prior to performing this test, students should feel comfortable and warm. Students may need to trial the different versions of the curl ups so that they know which one to select for the test. If music is used, it is recommended that the students practise performing some curl ups to the music to ensure that it encourages and permits a steady, continuous movement with good technique. This test could be carried out in pairs, with one student performing the test and their partner checking their technique and recording their score.

Test procedure

Curl up A
The student should lie on their back on a mat, with their head in contact with the mat, their knees bent and their feet flat and apart. The students' arms should be straight and resting on the floor, with their fingers towards their knees. Keeping their feet flat, the student curls up slowly, lifting their head and shoulders off the mat and sliding their fingertips forwards along the floor. The student then slowly curls back down again until his/her head touches the mat. The curl up movement should be continuous and controlled. The student stops when he/she can no longer continue, or their technique deteriorates, or he/she has completed 50 curl ups. The score is the number of continuous curl ups performed. The score should be recorded on the 'How fit are you?' record sheet.

Curl up B
The student should lie on their back on a mat, with their head in contact with the mat, their knees bent and their feet flat and apart. The students' arms should be bent with their elbows out and their hands at the side of

their head, fingers spread. Keeping their feet flat, the student curls up slowly, lifting their head and shoulders off the mat and keeping their elbows out. The student then slowly curls back down again until his/her head touches the mat. The curl up movement should be continuous and controlled. The student stops when he/she can no longer continue or their technique deteriorates or he/she has completed 50 curl ups. The score is the number of continuous curl ups performed. The score should be recorded on the 'How fit are you?' record sheet.

Recovery from test
Following the test, students should lengthen the abdominal muscles by performing a 'long, thin' stretch in which they aim to take their fingertips as far away from their toes as possible. The stretch can be performed lying down on a mat or standing, and should be held still for 10-20 seconds.

Push up
The push up test measures the muscular strength and endurance of the chest muscles (pectorals) and the muscles in the back of the upper arm (triceps). Two versions of push ups are described, an easier version (push up A) and a more demanding version (push up B).

Resources
Mat
CD player and music with a steady beat (about 120 bpm) (optional)
'How fit are you?' record sheet

Preparation for test
Prior to performing this test, students should feel comfortable and warm. Students may need to trial the different versions of the push ups so that they know which one to select for the test. If music is used, it is recommended that the students practise performing some push ups to the music to ensure that it encourages and permits a steady, continuous movement with good technique. As a guide, students should be able to perform 20 push ups a minute (with each push up taking three seconds to perform). This test could be carried out in pairs, with one student performing the test and their partner checking their technique and recording their score.

Test procedure

Push up A
The student should kneel on a mat, with their knees apart and toes tucked under. The student should lean forwards and place their hands under their shoulders with fingers flat, pointing away from their toes. The student should walk their hands forward until he/she is in a three-quarter push up position with their shoulders and hips in line. From this position, the student bends both arms until there is a 90 degree angle at the elbows, taking their chin down towards the floor, in front of their hands. The student then fully straightens their arms (without 'snapping' or 'locking out' at the elbows) to return to the starting position. The back should be straight throughout the test. The push up movement should be continuous and controlled. The student stops when he/she can no longer continue or their technique deteriorates or he/she has completed 50 push ups. The score is the number of continuous push ups performed. The score should be recorded on the 'How fit are you?' record sheet.

Push up B
The student should kneel on a mat, with their knees apart and toes tucked under. The student should lean forwards and place their hands under their shoulders with fingers flat, pointing away from their toes. The student should walk their hands forward until their legs are straight and their shoulders, hips and ankles are in line. From this position, the student bends both arms until there is a 90 degree angle at the elbows, taking their chin down towards the floor, in front of their hands. The student then fully straightens their arms (without 'snapping' or 'locking out' at the elbows) to return to the starting position. The back should be straight throughout the test. The push up movement should be continuous and controlled. The student stops when he/she can no longer continue or their technique deteriorates or he/she has completed 50 push ups. The score is the number of continuous push ups performed. The score should be recorded on the 'How fit are you?' record sheet.

Recovery from test
Following the test, students should lengthen the chest and upper arm muscles by performing pectorals and triceps stretches. The stretches can be performed sitting or standing, and each stretch should be held still for 10 to 20 seconds.

Flexibility

Flexibility refers to the range of movement around a joint. Good flexibility is important for health as it is associated with a reduced risk of poor posture, back pain and restrictions in movement.

Sit and reach

The sit and reach test predominantly measures the flexibility of the hamstring muscles in the back of the upper part of the legs. It also partially measures the flexibility of the muscles in the lower back.

Resources
Gym bench or sturdy box
String
Metre rule
Chalk
'How fit are you?' record sheet

Preparation for test
The muscles in the lower back and in the back of the legs (hamstrings) should be very warm before taking this test. It is recommended that students warm themselves up doing aerobic activities such as jogging and sidestepping. It would be appropriate for students to do the 'sit and reach' test immediately following the aerobic fitness test.

Test procedure
The sit and reach test requires a standard gym bench or a sturdy box approximately 30 centimetres high. The student sits down in front of the bench or box, with their backside, back and shoulders pressed up against a wall. Both legs are fully extended with feet flat against the end of the bench or box. The student extends both arms forward towards the bench/box with the hands placed palm down one directly on top of the other, and their backside, back and shoulders against the wall. Using a piece of string, the distance from the end of the student's fingers to the bench/box is measured, marked with chalk and recorded.

The student then leans gently forward reaching as far as possible with both hands along the top of the bench/box for at least one second. Again using a piece of string, the distance from the first mark to the end of the student's fingers along the bench/box is measured, marked and recorded.

Both legs should remain straight throughout the test and hips should remain square. Hands should reach forward evenly with one hand remaining directly over the other. The test should be repeated if the hips are not square, the hands reach unevenly, or the knees bend.

The student's score for the sit and reach test is the difference between the first score (with back pressed up against the wall) and the second score (leaning forwards as far as possible). Students should have two attempts at the test and the highest of the two scores recorded. This score should be recorded in centimetres on the 'How fit are you?' record sheet.

Recovery from test
Following this test, students should gently jog or walk until their back and leg muscles feel comfortable.

Guidance for your students following the tests

Appropriate responses to students about their fitness test scores include:

'If your fitness test score was in the healthy fitness range, congratulations. You are most likely doing regular physical activity and this is keeping you fit. If you are not, remember that being active is good fun and healthy.'

'If your fitness test score was not in the healthy fitness range, you might want to consider doing more physical activity to try to improve your health and fitness. If you are already active, well done, keep up the good work.'

References

The Abdominal Curl Conditioning Test CD Version (2003), Available from: Coachwise: www.1st4sport.com

The Cooper Institute. Meredith, M. D. and Welk, G. J. (eds) (2007), *FITNESSGRAM/ACTIVITYGRAM. Test Administration Manual, Fourth Edition*. Champaign, IL: Human Kinetics.

The Multistage Shuttle Run (1998), Available from: Coachwise: www.1st4sport.com

Physical Education Association (PEA). (1988), 'Health related fitness testing and monitoring in schools. A position statement on behalf of the PEA by its fitness and health advisory committee'. *British Journal of Physical Education*, **19**(4/5), pp. 194–5.

Appendix

How fit are you?

Complete a record of your scores on the following health-related fitness tests:

◆ Mini Bleep Test or Step Test
◆ Curl Up
◆ Push Up
◆ Sit and Reach

Your teacher will guide you through each of the tests.

The following tests are designed to measure the specified components of fitness which are associated with your health.

Fitness Test	Health-Related Component of Fitness	Associated Health Conditions
Mini Bleep Test or Step Test	Aerobic fitness	Coronary heart disease; obesity
Curl Ups and Push Ups	Muscular strength and endurance	Osteoporosis (fragile bones); back pain; poor posture
Sit and Reach	Flexibility	Back pain; limited range of movement; poor posture

Following the tests, compare your scores with the 'Healthy Fitness Ranges' and answer the 'Thinking about your Fitness' questions (see overleaf).

How Fit are You? Record

Name:

Year and Date	Mini Bleep Test	Is your score in the Healthy Fitness Range?	Step Test	Is your score in the Healthy Fitness Range?	Curl Ups	Is your score in the Healthy Fitness Range?	Push Ups	Is your score in the Healthy Fitness Range?	Sit and Reach	Is your score in the Healthy Fitness Range?
Year 7										
Year 8										
Year 9										
Year 10										
Year 11										

'Healthy Fitness Ranges'

Making Sense of your 'Fitness' Scores

Compare your scores with the 'Healthy Fitness Ranges' in the tables below.

Girls

Age	Mini Bleep Test (HR/15 seconds)	Step Test (HR/15 seconds)	Curl Ups	Push Ups	Sit and Reach
11	32–40	32–40	15–29	7–15	25
12	32–40	32–40	18–32	7–15	25
13	31–40	31–40	18–32	7–15	25
14	31–39	31–39	18–32	7–15	25
15	31–39	31–39	18–35	7–15	30
16	31–39	31–39	18–35	7–15	30
17	31–39	31–39	18–35	7–15	30
18	31–38	31–38	18–35	7–15	30

Boys

Age	Mini Bleep Test (HR/15 seconds)	Step Test (HR/15 seconds)	Curl Ups	Push Ups	Sit and Reach
11	32–40	32–40	15–28	8–20	20
12	32–40	32–40	18–36	10–20	20
13	31–40	31–40	21–40	12–25	20
14	31–39	31–39	24–45	14–30	20
15	31–39	31–39	24–47	16–35	20
16	31–39	31–39	24–47	18–35	20
17	31–39	31–39	24–47	18–35	20
18	31–38	31–38	24–47	18–35	20

Thinking about your Fitness

◆ What does your 'aerobic fitness' score tell you?

_____

_____

◆ What does your 'muscular strength and endurance' score tell you?

_____

_____

◆ What does your 'flexibility' score tell you?

_____

_____

◆ Are you fit enough for your age?

_____

_____

◆ Do you think you need to become fitter? If yes, in which areas of fitness?

_____

_____

◆ How could you go about being fitter?

_____

_____

◆ State three actions you could carry out over the next few months to improve your fitness.

_____

_____

→ _continued_

◆ What will help you to carry out these actions?

_____

_____

◆ What might prevent you from carrying out these actions?

_____

_____

◆ On a scale of 0–10, how confident are you that you will be able to increase your fitness levels over the next few months?

Not at all confident   Very confident

1 _____ 10

6 | Establishing how active children are

Introduction

While a good deal of attention has been paid to monitoring children's physical fitness, relatively little attention has been given to monitoring their physical activity. In this chapter then, we focus primarily on physical activity monitoring. Given our plea in Chapter 5 to focus more on the process of physical activity rather than the product of fitness, and the limitations and issues with fitness testing, we feel that physical activity monitoring is an important, extremely useful, yet underused and often neglected means of monitoring children and promoting physical activity.

As we did for physical fitness, first we consider the purposes for and main methods of monitoring. We then present some ideas for implementing physical activity monitoring with your students. Finally, we offer some suggestions for alternative but equally appropriate ways in which you might monitor your students' progress in this area.

The purpose of monitoring physical activity

Monitoring physical activity can serve a number of purposes within school. These include the following:

◆ to establish how active students are;
◆ to establish whether students are meeting physical activity recommendations (see Chapter 4);
◆ to determine the effectiveness of initiatives and strategies designed to increase physical activity;
◆ meeting the National Curriculum for Physical Education requirements. If pupils are to understand the concept of 'healthy, active lifestyles' and develop the skills and processes to 'make informed choices about healthy, active lifestyles' and 'develop physical and

mental capacity', then they clearly need to be aware of how active they are and should be and how they can determine this. This requires them to know how to make informed assessments of their physical activity behaviour;

◆ to address calls to focus more on physical activity as a desirable outcome than on fitness (see Chapters 2 and 5 for this debate).

Methods of monitoring physical activity

More than 30 different methods of assessing physical activity are available which can be grouped into different categories. Here we provide a brief overview only of the methods that we consider might be useful and feasible for you to use with your students in school. For easy reference, the major strengths and limitations of each method are summarized in Table 6.1. Broadly, the methods can be categorized as follows:

◆ self-and/or proxy report;
◆ physiological – heart-rate monitoring;
◆ motion sensors – movement counters or pedometers and accelerometers;
◆ observation.

Self-and/or proxy report

Self-report is probably the most commonly used method of monitoring children's physical activity. Self-report measures suitable for use with children include self-completion questionnaires, interviewer-administered questionnaires, diaries and proxy reports (in which parents or teachers report on the child's activity using any of the formats).

Measures vary in detail, the type of information they collect (e.g. type, duration, intensity and frequency of physical activity), in the period of time covered by the report (e.g. one year, one week, one day), and in how the results are reported (e.g. as activity scores, time or minutes spent in activity).

A variety of self-report measures have been developed for use with children but it is also possible to develop your own questionnaire. We include some example questionnaires for you towards the end of this chapter.

Physiological

Heart-rate monitoring – There is a strong link between heart rate and energy expenditure during exercise, which makes heart-rate monitoring a useful method of assessing physical activity. Heart-rate monitoring has often been used to estimate children's daily activity. A number of self-contained, computerized telemetry systems have been developed in recent years which consist of a lightweight transmitter, fixed to the chest with electrodes, and a receiver/microcomputer which is worn as a wrist-watch. Perhaps the most well-known, commercially available and affordable of these is the Polar Sports tester.

Motion sensors

Movement counters or pedometers – The simplest form of motion sensor which can be used with children is the pedometer, often called a step counter, which literally counts the number of steps the child takes as an indicator of the total amount of physical activity. The pedometer can also provide an estimate of the distance walked by entering a measure of stride length, and some can provide a crude estimate of energy expenditure if body weight is entered into the device. It is generally worn on the hip or waist and relies on vertical movements of the body to trigger a switch each time a step is taken.

Accelerometers – Accelerometers are more sophisticated electronic devices that measure accelerations produced by the child's movement. They are also usually worn on the hip and convert body accelerations to an activity count. A number of accelerometers are now available that vary in complexity and cost.

Observation

Observation measures physical activity directly and is particularly well suited to children. It involves watching physical activity, recording it (either on a coding form or through a handheld computer device), and then converting the record into some type of summary score. Various instruments for the systematic observation of children's physical activity have been developed for use in school and physical education lessons, as well as in general settings.

Table 6.1 Physical activity monitoring methods and their main strengths and limitations

Methods	Description	Strengths	Limitations
Self-report	• Includes questionnaires, interviewer-administered questionnaires and diaries. • Vary in detail, type of activity information collected (e.g. type, duration, intensity, frequency), the time covered (e.g. one year/week/day) and in how results are reported (e.g. activity scores, time/minutes in activity). • A variety of children's measures are available but teachers can develop their own.	• Convenient, time and cost efficient. • Can provide detailed physical activity information. • Not burdensome. • Non-reactive (i.e. do not alter physical activity behaviour).	• Accuracy, validity and reliability. • Problems with memory, interpretation, honesty. • Can be a burden (if long/complicated). • Not very appropriate for all types of activity (e.g. unstructured play).
Heart-rate monitor	• Provides a useful estimate of physical activity. • A lightweight transmitter fixed to the chest with electrodes, and a receiver worn as a wrist-watch. • The most well-known, commercially available heart-rate monitor is the Polar Sports tester.	• Small, relatively cheap, robust, easy to use, socially acceptable. • Unobtrusive/does not restrict movement. • Does not influence 'normal' activity. • Information can be collected for long periods. • Reliable and valid.	• Not a direct measure of activity. • Other factors influence heart rate (e.g. metabolism, emotions, temperature, type of exercise, fitness level). • Possible interference/loss of signal. • May be uncomfortable to wear. • How to summarize/use the information.
Pedometer	• A step counter which counts the number of steps taken as a measure of physical activity. • Can provide an estimate of distance walked (by entering stride length) and an estimate of energy expenditure (by entering body weight). • Usually worn on the hip.	• Small, relatively cheap, easy to use, socially acceptable. • Unobtrusive/does not restrict movement. • Does not influence 'normal' activity. • Becoming more reliable and valid.	• Provides limited activity information. • Does not measure activity intensity. • Cannot be used for all activities (e.g. cycling, rowing). • Energy expenditure calculation is inaccurate.

Methods	Description	Strengths	Limitations
Accelerometer	• A more sophisticated (electronic) device. • Measures and converts body accelerations to an activity count as a measure of physical activity. • Usually worn on the hip. • A number are available that vary in complexity and cost.	• As for pedometer.	• Provides limited activity information. • Cannot be used for all activities (e.g. static exercise such as gym work).
Observation	• Involves watching and recording activity (via a form/computer), and converting the record into a summary score. • Various methods have been developed for use in school/physical education lessons.	• A direct measure of physical activity. • Can provide accurate, detailed information. • Appropriate for children's activity (which is sporadic, transitory). • Observers can be trained quickly. • Reliable and valid.	• Activity recorded is limited to what is seen (may miss information). • Limits to where and when activity can be observed. • Reactivity of children (i.e. altering behaviour due to being observed). • Burdensome and time intensive for observer.

Implementing physical activity monitoring with your students

There are then a number of different measures to choose from if wishing to monitor your students' physical activity levels. As Table 6.1 shows, all methods have strengths and limitations. In selecting and using any measure, you should consider these, as well as the reason(s) for your assessment and the number and age of your students.

For research purposes, gaining an accurate measure of physical activity is important and using a combination of, or multiple methods has therefore been recommended in order to provide a more accurate and complete picture of children's activity levels. When choosing a measure of physical activity for use with your students, the accuracy researchers try to achieve is not required. Instead, issues such as cost, ease of use and educational value are more important and the limitations should not be seen to devalue the assessment. Rather than worrying about the precision of the method you use, we believe it is more important to ensure that your students learn from the experience.

Now that we have identified those measures that we feel are useful and feasible for you to use with your students, we present some ideas as to how these methods might be incorporated within physical education.

Heart-rate monitoring

Heart-rate monitors are now frequently used in the physical education curriculum to help students learn about the cardiovascular system and target heart ranges but they could also be used to monitor selected students' heart rates and therefore activity levels during lessons, over a school day, or for a more extended period of time (e.g. a school week, a unit of work). The data could then be shared and discussed. Cost may prohibit your school from purchasing multiple sophisticated heart-rate monitors and therefore collecting and analysing data on large numbers, but a few such monitors could be used effectively within and beyond physical education. Simple heart-rate monitors are also now available which are much more affordable and which could be used on a larger scale.

Motion sensors

As with heart-rate monitors, cost may be an issue with some motion sensors. Basic pedometers, however, can be purchased at a relatively low cost and could be used with your students in much the same way as heart-rate monitors.

Observation

Valuable physical activity information can be obtained by observation without you having to use sophisticated methods. Simple observation sheets could be prepared on which all details of activity (e.g. type, intensity, duration) could be recorded. Your students could be asked to observe and record the physical activity of one of their classmates during a school day or week, which would involve tracking their peer's movements during lessons, break times, lunch times and after school. The information recorded could then be shared and discussed.

Self-report

Self-report probably offers the greatest potential for use in the curriculum and is likely to be the most practical and easiest method for you to incorporate into lessons. You could use an existing questionnaire (see examples later in this chapter), or devise a questionnaire of your own to meet your own and your students' needs, adapting or using the questions below as a guide to developing your own form.

A quick and simple indication of your students' activity levels can be gained by asking general questions about their physical activity. For example:

During a 7-day period (a week), how many times on average do you do the following kind of physical activity?

- ◆ Vigorous – activity that involves lots of effort and makes your heart beat fast such as basketball, football, jogging/running, energetic dancing, aerobics or circuit training.
- ◆ Moderate – activity that makes you warm and slightly out of breath but not exhausted, such as brisk walking, steady swimming, cycling or dancing.
- ◆ Light – activity that involves little effort, such as walking, bowling or snooker.

Another example is:

	No	1–2	3–4	5–6	7 times or more
Do you do any of the following physical activities? If yes, usually how many times per week?					
Skipping	0	0	0	0	0
Tag	0	0	0	0	0
Walking	0	0	0	0	0
Cycling	0	0	0	0	0
Jogging or running	0	0	0	0	0
Aerobics	0	0	0	0	0
Swimming	0	0	0	0	0
Dance	0	0	0	0	0
Football	0	0	0	0	0
Badminton	0	0	0	0	0
Skateboarding	0	0	0	0	0
Soccer	0	0	0	0	0
Basketball	0	0	0	0	0
etc.					

Two example questionnaires that you might wish to administer to your students follow. The first questionnaire requires students to recall their activity over a period of a week, whereas the second asks students to record their activity for one school day and one day at the weekend. Both forms assume that the activity the students record is typical of their usual or habitual physical activity. The second questionnaire also includes a number of useful follow-up 'Thinking about your Physical Activity' questions which can be used as a discussion point with your students. They also link well to the physical activity recommendations for young people we looked at in Chapter 4.

Example physical activity questionnaire

Physical Activity Questionnaire

How much physical activity did you do last week?

Did you do you any light, moderate or vigorous activity? If so, how much?

Light activity involves little effort (e.g. walking, bowling or snooker)

Moderate activity makes you warm and slightly out of breath but not exhausted (e.g. brisk walking, steady swimming, cycling or dancing)

Vigorous activity involves lots of effort and makes your heart beat fast (e.g. basketball, football, jogging/running, energetic dancing, aerobics or circuit training)

Instructions

Record any physical activity that you did **last week** in the table.

Start with yesterday and take each day one at a time until you record all the activity you did in the last week.

Record the **name of the activity** (e.g. football, walking) and **how many minutes** you did the activity for (e.g. 15 minutes, 60 minutes) in the correct column according to whether you did it in the **morning, afternoon or evening** and whether it was **light, moderate or vigorous**.

Read the descriptions of light, moderate and vigorous activity above. Write the activity(ies) above the line and the number of minutes below. For example:

Brisk walking
_____
30 minutes

Then, add up how much moderate and/or vigorous activity you did last week.

	Yesterday Day 1	Day 2	Day 3	Day 4	Day 5	Day 6	Last Week Day 7
Morning							
Light	——	——	——	——	——	——	——
Moderate	——	——	——	——	——	——	——
Vigorous	——	——	——	——	——	——	——
Afternoon							
Light	——	——	——	——	——	——	——
Moderate	——	——	——	——	——	——	——
Vigorous	——	——	——	——	——	——	——
Evening							
Light	——	——	——	——	——	——	——
Moderate	——	——	——	——	——	——	——
Vigorous	——	——	——	——	——	——	——
Total daily moderate activity =							
Total daily vigorous activity =							
						Total weekly moderate activity =	
						Total weekly vigorous activity =	
						Total weekly moderate/ vigorous activity =	

Example physical activity questionnaire

How active are you?

Record your physical activity for one school day and one day at the weekend.

You need to:

◆ describe each physical activity you do
◆ decide whether each activity was:
  1. **light**: which feels easy and involves only a small increase in breathing rate and heart rate
  2. **moderate**: which feels energetic and makes you feel warm and slightly out of breath
  3. **vigorous**: which feels very energetic and involves large increases in breathing rate and heart rate
◆ record the number of minutes you spent doing each physical activity
◆ add up the total number of minutes you were active each day
◆ answer the 'Thinking about your Physical Activity' questions.

Date of school day:

Part of school day	Activity (e.g. cycling, walking, hockey, dancing)	Light (L), Moderate (M) or Vigorous (V)	Number of minutes
Before school			
Morning lessons			
Morning break			
Lessons after break			
Lunch time			
Afternoon lessons			
After school			
Evening			
		Total minutes of moderate and vigorous activity	

Date of weekend day:

Time	Activity (e.g. cycling, walking, hockey, dancing)	Light (L), Moderate (M) or Vigorous (V)	Number of minutes
7–9am			
9–11am			
11am–1pm			
1–3pm			
3–5pm			
5–7pm			
7–9pm			
9–11pm			
		Total minutes of moderate and vigorous activity	

Thinking about your Physical Activity

◆ Did you take part in at least ONE HOUR of moderate and/or vigorous activity on your school day?

_____

_____

◆ Was this a normal school day? If not, please explain why.

_____

_____

◆ Did you take part in at least ONE HOUR of moderate and/or vigorous activity on your weekend day?

_____

_____

◆ Was this a normal weekend day? If not, please explain why.

_____

_____

◆ Are you more active on school days or weekend days? Why do you think this is?

_____

_____

◆ Are the activities you usually do of at least moderate intensity (e.g. the activity feels 'energetic' or 'very energetic')?

_____

_____

→ *continued*

◆ Do the activities you usually do include exercises to improve your strength and flexibility?

_____

_____

◆ Are you active enough for your age? (i.e. do you do ONE HOUR or more of at least moderate intensity activity each day, including some strength and flexibility exercise at least twice a week?)

_____

_____

◆ Do you think you should become more active? If yes, what is your target?

_____

_____

◆ If yes, how can you achieve this target?

_____

_____

◆ State three actions you could carry out over the next three months to increase your activity levels.

_____

_____

◆ What will help you to carry out these actions?

_____

_____

→ _continued_

◆ **What might prevent you from carrying out these actions?**

_____

_____

◆ On a scale of 0–10, how confident are you that you will be able to increase your activity levels over the next three months?

Not at all confident   Very confident

1 _____ 10

Computer-based physical activity questionnaires are also becoming popular and may be an attractive option to use with your students. For example, ACTIVITYGRAM (which also forms part of FITNESS-GRAM/ACTIVITYGRAM which was described in Chapter 5), is a physical activity assessment programme which is designed to assess and compute the type and amount of moderate or vigorous physical activity students perform each day over three days. The software provides individualized report cards as well as record keeping functions to help students evaluate their physical activity patterns and learn self-monitoring skills to help them be active in later life. The report cards also provide recommendations to assist students in finding ways to be more active.

Finally, another idea would be for you to ask your students to keep physical activity diaries for a specified period of time, or complete Records of Achievement (ROA) or Student Profiles designed to include space for students to record details of their involvement in physical activity in and out of school.

Using the physical activity information

As with fitness, monitoring your students' physical activity should not just be another data gathering exercise. Having obtained the physical activity data, we suggest that it can and should be used in a variety of practical ways, as outlined below.

1. To enhance your students' knowledge and understanding of physical activity concepts (e.g. the importance of physical activity (see Chapter 1), that moderate activity is good for health (see Chapter 4), what the constraints/barriers to participation are and how these can be overcome (see Chapter 3)).

2. To develop your students' personal activity knowledge (e.g. about their current activity levels) and self-evaluation skills (e.g. to enable them to plan and make decisions about their physical activity) (see the earlier questionnaire 'Thinking about your Physical Activity').

3. To facilitate goal setting and self-monitoring of physical activity by your students (e.g. using the information as the basis for setting realistic goals to increase or maintain their physical activity levels and/or to work towards meeting physical activity recommendations for young people (see Chapter 4 and the 'Thinking about your Physical Activity' questions in Figure 6.2).

4. To diagnose students' activity needs for individual exercise prescription (e.g. to establish whether a student is meeting current physical activity recommendations and therefore what his/her activity needs are).

5. To promote personalized learning and thinking skills in your students through physical education (e.g. independent enquiry, reflection, self-managing, effective participation), cross-curricular dimensions (e.g. identity, healthy lifestyles, critical thinking) or links with other subjects (e.g. handling, presenting and interpreting data in mathematics).

Alternative monitoring methods

If children are to be encouraged to focus on the process of activity, as well as, or in place of the product of fitness, then this should be reflected in the assessment methods that are used. As we said in Chapter 5, you may decide to abandon fitness testing in favour of monitoring physical activity. But, even if you employ both fitness and activity monitoring with your students, we still recommend that you use other forms of assessment alongside.

Student achievement in this area is not limited to their performance or engagement in activity and fitness, but relates also to improvements in:

- knowledge and understanding;
- competence and motor skills;
- attitudes and confidence.

You may monitor these in your students through:

- responses to focused questions (student–teacher or student–student) and practical tasks;
- teacher observation of student performance in practical tasks;
- students taking more responsibility for their actions within and outside of lessons;
- students' attendance, participation and commitment in physical education lessons;
- students' participation and commitment in out-of-school-hours activities;
- students' participation in physical activity beyond school.

Examples of the above include:

- student answers (student–teacher or student–student) to the following focused questions (appropriate for specific Key Stages):
  - Which muscles are working hard when you run? (Key Stages 2/3)
  - Why is it important to stretch muscles after you have worked them? (Key Stages 2/3)
  - How much activity is recommended for young people? (Key Stage 3)
  - Explain how stronger upper body muscles help you to throw further (Key Stage 4)
  - What are some of the main reasons why young people are not active? (Key Stage 4)
- student responses to the following tasks (appropriate for specific Key Stages):
  - Show me a stretch for the muscles in the back of your leg (Key Stages 2/3)
  - Perform an exercise which will strengthen your abdominal muscles (Key Stage 3)
  - For next week's lesson, make a list of the different places in the local area where you could be active (other than at school) (Key Stage 3)
- student entries in activity diaries or ROA (e.g. keeping a record for

a number of weeks of all the activity, sport, dance and exercise performed at school, home, travelling, in the local area);

◆ the proportion of physical education lessons missed and/or not participated in by a student;

◆ the degree of interest shown and effort put into physical education lessons;

◆ student involvement in out-of-school-hours clubs, practices, activities and events;

◆ student involvement in clubs, activities and events beyond school.

III | How? – The Curriculum

7 | The physical education curriculum

Introduction

As we highlighted in Chapter 1, physical education and physical education teachers are recognized as having a key role to play in promoting healthy, active lifestyles in children. In particular, the area of 'health and fitness' or health-related exercise (HRE) within the curriculum has the role of providing appropriate physical activity opportunities, information and guidance to children, and encouraging and empowering them to make informed lifestyle choices. Here we consider how, through the physical education curriculum, and specifically HRE, you can promote and achieve the above. We look at some of the key developments that we feel are of interest and relevance, and then at the interpretation, philosophy, content, organization and delivery of HRE.

Developments

In recent years there have been a number of positive developments that have implications for physical education and real potential to enhance the provision and quality of HRE and the promotion of physical activity in schools generally.

Maintaining health through physical education is not a new idea and physical education was driven by this objective at the beginning of the twentieth century. However, by the end of the Second World War other objectives of physical education became more important and attention shifted more towards self-discovery and the acquisition of physical skills. It was not until the early 1980s that health once again became important. Since this time, the emphasis and interest has grown to the point that most schools now incorporate health-based programmes within their physical education curriculum.

The National Curriculum for Physical Education

Of course, a key development that has helped to promote and re-establish the area has been the National Curriculum for Physical Education (NCPE). HRE has been included as a statutory component of the NCPE since its introduction in 1992 and has also featured within the Personal, Social and Health Education (formerly Health Education) curriculum. As a result, HRE is now formally recognized and has a specific place and knowledge base in the curriculum. Furthermore, a stronger emphasis on health-related issues has been provided with each revision of the NCPE.

The new Secondary National Curriculum for England (QCA, 2007) comprises a statutory programme of study for physical education at Key Stages 3 and 4 as well as non-statutory programmes of study for personal, social, and health education: personal well-being for both Key Stages. These, as with the programmes of study for all subjects, comprise an 'importance statement', 'key concepts', 'key processes', a 'range and content' or breadth of study, and 'curriculum opportunities'.

In terms of HRE and the coverage of health-related issues, 'healthy, active lifestyles' is a key concept and 'making informed choices about healthy, active lifestyles' and 'developing physical and mental capacity' are key processes within the new Secondary NCPE. Furthermore, 'exercising safely and effectively to improve health and well-being, as in fitness and health activities' also represents one of the six areas within the 'range and content' at both Key Stages 3 and 4 and from which teachers should draw when teaching the key concepts and processes. Examples of other areas include outwitting opponents, as in games activities; accurate replication of actions, phrases and sequences, as in gymnastic activities; and exploring and communicating ideas, concepts and emotions, as in dance activities. Under 'curriculum opportunities', the curriculum at Key Stages 3 and 4 should also provide opportunities for pupils to get involved in a broad range of different activities that develop the whole body. Tables 7.1 and 7.2 summarize the key HRE requirements of the new Secondary NCPE for Key Stages 3 and 4 (QCA, 2007).

Table 7.1 The Key HRE Requirements of the New Secondary NCPE – Key Stage 3

Key Concept	Key Process	Key Process	Range and Content	Curriculum Opportunities
Healthy, active lifestyles	Developing physical and mental capacity	Making informed choices about healthy, active lifestyles	Exercising safely and effectively to improve health and well-being, as in fitness and health activities	The curriculum should provide opportunities for pupils to:
Involves pupils:	Pupils should be able to:	Pupils should be able to:		
• Understanding that physical activity contributes to the healthy functioning of the body and mind and is an essential component of a healthy lifestyle.	• develop their physical strength, stamina, speed and flexibility to cope with the demands of different activities • develop their mental determination to succeed.	• identify the types of activity they are best suited to • identify the types of role they would like to take on • make choices about their involvement in healthy physical activity.	Represents one area of six, at least four of which should be covered. Exercising safely and effectively includes activities such as aqua aerobics, weight training, jogging and power walking, in which success is related to improving feelings of health, fitness and well-being. Goals might include emotional well-being, healthy weight management, toned muscles, healthy skin and a healthy heart.	• get involved in a broad range of different activities that, in combination, develop the whole body. This includes activities that develop the strength, stamina, suppleness and speed of the upper body and arms, and lower body and legs. This can be achieved through at least two hours of focused weekly activities in curriculum time.
• Recognizing that regular physical activity that is fit for purpose, safe and enjoyable has the greatest impact on physical, mental and social well-being.	Physical strength, stamina, speed and flexibility includes: • strength to deal with the efforts and loads placed on the body • stamina to maintain effort (both cardiovascular and muscular) • speed to contract muscles quickly and slowly	The above includes regularly getting involved in physical education, sport, dance and healthy physical activity. It supports government aspirations for pupils to have at least two hours per week of high-quality physical education and school sport delivered within the		• follow pathways to other activities in and beyond school.

Table 7.1 (Contd)

Key Concept	Key Process	Key Process	Key Process	Range and Content	Curriculum Opportunities
Healthy, active lifestyles	Developing physical and mental capacity	Making informed choices about healthy, active lifestyles		Exercising safely and effectively to improve health and well-being, as in fitness and health activities	The curriculum should provide opportunities for pupils to:
Involves pupils:	Pupils should be able to:	Pupils should be able to:	curriculum, and an additional two hours beyond the school day delivered by a range of school, community and club providers.		This may involve: • regularly getting involved in physical education, sport, dance and healthy physical activity • taking part in school and community sport and dance opportunities, etc.
	• flexibility to move joints through their full range. Mental determination includes: • the confidence to have a go • the determination to face up to challenges and keep going • expressing and dealing with emotions • success for oneself and others.				

Table 7.2 The Key HRE Requirements of the New Secondary NCPE – Key Stage 4

Key Concept	Key Process	Key Process	Range and Content	Curriculum Opportunities
Healthy, active lifestyles	Developing physical and mental capacity	Making informed choices about healthy, active lifestyles	Exercising safely and effectively to improve health and well-being, as in fitness and health activities	The curriculum should provide opportunities for pupils to:
Involves pupils:	Pupils should be able to:	Pupils should be able to:		
• Understanding that physical activity contributes to the healthy functioning of the body and mind and is an essential component of a healthy lifestyle. • Recognizing that regular physical activity that is fit for purpose, safe and enjoyable has the greatest impact on physical, mental and social well-being.	• analyse how mental and physical capacity affects performance • maintain and develop their physical strength, stamina, speed and flexibility to cope with the demands of different activities and active lifestyles • prepare mentally for successful involvement in physical activity, performance and engagement in healthy, active lifestyles. Physical strength, stamina, speed and flexibility includes: • strength to deal with the efforts and loads placed on the body • stamina to maintain effort (cardiovascular and muscular) • speed to contract muscles quickly and slowly • flexibility to move joints through their full range • balance to maintain control, shape and alignment	• identify the types of physical activity available to them and the roles they would like to take on • link physical activity with diet, work and rest for personal health and well-being • make informed decisions about getting involved in a lifetime of healthy physical activities that suit their needs. The above includes maintaining and increasing their involvement in physical education, sport, dance and healthy physical	Represents one area of six, at least two of which should be covered. Exercising safely and effectively includes activities such as aqua aerobics, weight training, jogging and power walking, in which success is related to improving feelings of health, fitness and well-being. Goals might include emotional well-being, healthy weight management, toned muscles, healthy skin and a healthy heart.	• get involved in a broad range of different activities that, in combination, develop the whole body. This includes activities that develop the strength, stamina, suppleness and speed of the upper body and arms, and lower body and legs. This can be achieved through at least two hours of focused weekly activities in curriculum time. • follow pathways to other activities in and beyond school.

Table 7.2 (contd)

Key Concept	Key Process	Key Process	Range and Content	Curriculum Opportunities
Healthy, active lifestyles	Developing physical and mental capacity	Making informed choices about healthy, active lifestyles	Exercising safely and effectively to improve health and well-being, as in fitness and health activities	The curriculum should provide opportunities for pupils to:
Involves pupils:	Pupils should be able to: • co-ordination for balanced and effective interaction of movements • agility to move quickly and nimbly • using aerobic and anaerobic body systems • understanding what their bodies can and cannot do as they go through periods of change and development • understanding the benefits of training and preparing for activity and the types of general and specific training methods. Prepare mentally includes: • the place of motivation, anxiety, arousal and tension in effective performance • the confidence to get involved • the determination to face up to challenges and keep going • expressing and dealing with emotions • the desire to achieve success for oneself and others.	Pupils should be able to: activity to meet government targets for physical education, school sport and club links.		This may involve: • regularly getting involved in physical education, sport, dance and healthy physical activity • taking part in school and community sport and dance opportunities, etc.

The National Curriculum for Wales is similar, comprising programmes of study for physical education and a framework for personal and aocial education. However, the NCPE in Wales identifies 'health, fitness and well-being activities' as one of four areas of experience which must be taught at Key Stages 2, 3 and 4.

Guidance material

While the NCPE has required health issues to be taught since its introduction, its goal, philosophy, content, organization and delivery has and still is not always well understood. Elsewhere we have reported that there has been limited systematic expression of health in physical education, much variation in practice, and inconsistent and insufficient guidance for teachers about the teaching of HRE in physical education.

To address these concerns, a Health-Related Exercise Working group was established in 1997 in an effort to establish a consensus approach to the area. The group comprised representatives from schools, higher education, the advisory service, and key sport, health and physical education organizations, and their main task was to produce good practice guidelines for teachers in the form of a curriculum resource. After consultation, the following resource was produced by Jo Harris in 2000: *Health-Related Exercise in the National Curriculum. Key Stages 1 to 4*, published by Human Kinetics (see References).

This text remains a valuable resource for all teachers involved in teaching HRE. It contains guidance on:

◆ Terminology
◆ Rationale and physical activity recommendations
◆ Delivery and assessment
◆ Requirements and approaches
◆ Schemes and units of work.

Under the requirements section in the book you will find an interpretation of the National Curriculum requirements for health and fitness for Curriculum 2000 (DfES and QCA, 1999). The interpretation is expressed in the form of learning outcomes for each Key Stage within physical education and incorporates links with relevant health-related aspects of personal, social and health education and science. Whilst the interpretation is based on Curriculum 2000, the learning outcomes are still considered to be relevant and applicable to the new Secondary NCPE (QCA, 2007). To clarify the range of coverage and the progression between Key Stages, the outcomes have been placed into four categories:

◆ Safety issues
◆ Exercise effects
◆ Health benefits
◆ Activity promotion

Example learning outcomes under each of these categories include:

◆ Safety issues
  Key Stage 3 – Demonstrate an understanding of safe exercise practices (e.g. tying long hair back and removing jewellery to avoid injury; adopting good posture when sitting, standing and moving; performing exercises with good technique; washing or showering following energetic activity; using equipment and facilities with permission and, where necessary, under supervision; administering basic first aid).
  Key Stage 4 – Be able to recognize and manage risk and apply safe exercise principles and procedures (e.g. not exercising when unwell or injured; avoiding prolonged high-impact exercise; administering first aid, including resuscitation techniques; avoiding excessive amounts of exercise).
◆ Exercise effects
  Key Stage 3 – Understand and monitor a range of short-term effects of exercise on the body systems: (i) cardiovascular system (e.g. changes in breathing and heart rate, temperature, appearance, feelings, recovery rate, ability to pace oneself and remain within a target zone); (ii) musculo-skeletal system (e.g. increases in muscular strength, endurance and flexibility; improved muscle tone and posture; enhanced functional capacity and sport or dance performance).
  Key Stage 4 – Know and understand that training programmes develop both health-related components (cardiovascular fitness, muscular strength and endurance, flexibility, body composition, composure, decision-making) and skill-related components of physical and mental fitness (agility, balance, co-ordination, power, reaction time, speed, concentration, determination).
◆ Health benefits
  Key Stage 3 – Know and understand a range of long-term benefits of exercise on physical health: (i) reduced risk of chronic disease

(e.g. heart disease); (ii) reduced risk of bone disease (e.g. osteoporosis); (iii) reduced risk of some health conditions (e.g. obesity, back pain); (iv) improved management of some health conditions (e.g. asthma, diabetes, arthritis).
Key Stage 4 – Know and understand that frequent and appropriate exercise enhances the physical, social and psychological well-being of all individuals including the young and old, disabled and non-disabled, and those with health conditions (e.g. asthma, depression) and chronic disease (e.g. arthritis).

◆ Activity promotion
Key Stage 3 – Be able to access information about a range of activity opportunities at school, home and in the local community and know ways of incorporating exercise into their lifestyles (e.g. walking or cycling to school or to meet friends, helping around the home or garden).
Key Stage 4 – Be able to plan, perform, monitor and evaluate a safe and effective health-related exercise programme that meets their personal needs and preferences over an extended period (e.g. over 6 to 12 weeks).

Young and Active?

Another important development was the launch of the Health Education Authority's (now the Health Development Agency) policy framework for the promotion of health-enhancing physical activity for young people, 'Young and Active?', in June 1998 (see Chapter 4 for further details). In addition to providing a review of the evidence available on young people and physical activity and physical activity recommendations, this framework identified the education sector as having a key role to play in promoting health-enhancing physical activity and included a series of recommendations as to how schools can promote physical activity to young people.

Government policies

Finally, and as was mentioned in Chapter 1, the role of schools and physical education in promoting health and encouraging participation in sport and physical activity have been a focus of government policy in recent years. The most recent and notable examples include Every Child Matters and the Physical Education and Sport Strategy for Young People (formerly PESSCL) (we look at the latter in detail in Chapter 13).

The government's long-term ambition for 2010, referred to as the 'five hours a week' target, is:

To ensure that all children should have two hours of curriculum physical education and the opportunity to access a further two to three hours of sport beyond the curriculum per week.

To achieve this, we are witnessing continued substantial financial investment by government in physical education and school sport, through a whole host of initiatives and programmes (see Chapter 13 for details).

HRE interpretation and philosophy

We have often found that HRE means different things to different people. In Chapter 1 we provided a definition to explain what HRE was, but perhaps we also need to explain what it is not! To recap, HRE relates to:

the teaching of knowledge, understanding, physical competence and behavioural skills, and the creation of positive attitudes and confidence associated with current and lifelong participation in physical activity.

HRE is physical activity associated with health enhancement and should involve learning through active participation in purposeful activity embracing a range of sport, dance and exercise experiences including individualized lifetime activities.

Misunderstandings however, have sometimes led to narrow interpretations such as that HRE involves:

◆ vigorous activity such as cross-country running (in which young people are forced to 'huff and puff' or 'heave and pull');
◆ fitness testing;
◆ safety and hygiene issues (e.g. warming up and cooling down, lifting and carrying equipment, showers);
◆ 'boring' theory.

We stress that HRE is not the above. In fact, these interpretations are worrying because they could lead to undesirable practices in physical education such as forced fitness regimes, uninspiring drills, repetitive, directed activity which involves little or no learning, or inactive physical education lessons involving too much theory or teacher talk.

On the one hand, some teachers might get 'bogged down' in theory, whereas others might ignore or fail to recognize the knowledge base associated with HRE and deliver purely activity-based units (e.g. blocks of aerobics or cross-country) in which there is little or no development of students' knowledge and understanding.

Also, the thinking that HRE is simply a matter of delivering information and knowledge to students and telling them to be more active is a mistake. Knowledge alone is insufficient to bring about changes because it ignores the other important influences on children's physical activity that we discussed in Chapter 3, such as social and cultural influences and the environment.

The above approaches are obviously unhelpful and are unlikely to be successful in terms of promoting physical activity to your students. Instead, some of the key guiding principles that underpin the area and that we feel you should share with your students are:

◆ exercise can be a positive and enjoyable experience;
◆ exercise is for all;
◆ everyone can benefit from exercise;
◆ everyone can be good at exercise;
◆ everyone can find the right kind of exercise for them;
◆ exercise is for life;
◆ excellence in HRE is maintaining an active way of life.

Organization

The National Curriculum outlines the content to be taught, not the method of delivery. This allows you and your school scope to use your professional judgement to decide how best to teach the key concepts and processes relating to 'healthy, active lifestyles' and 'physical and mental capacity', and through which practical activities. Your responsibility and that of your department is to deliver the statutory requirements of the NCPE effectively. In our opinion, the critical issue should be the effectiveness of your students' learning and not the particular approach you adopt.

Despite this, there has and continues to be much discussion concerning the way in which HRE should be organized within the curriculum. In order for you and your department to make an informed decision about which approach or approaches to adopt, we encourage you to consider all the options available. The different approaches to choose from include:

◆ permeation or integration
◆ focused or discrete
◆ topic
◆ combined or mixed.

The strengths and limitations of each are described for you in Table 7.3.

Table 7.3 The approaches to delivering HRE

Approach	Strengths	Limitations
Permeation/integration An approach in which HRE is taught soley through other areas of physical education (e.g. games, athletics, dance, outdoor and adventurous activities).	HRE knowledge, understanding and skills can be seen as part of and integral to all physical education experiences. Children learn that all physical activities can contribute towards good health and can become part of an active lifestyle.	HRE knowledge, understanding and skills may become lost or marginalized amongst other information relating to skills and performance; and/or pupils may be overloaded with information. Much liaison activity is required to ensure that all pupils receive similar information from different teachers. The approach may be somewhat ad hoc and piecemeal.
Focused/discrete An approach involving teaching HRE through specific focused lessons or units of work (e.g. on fitness and health activities) either within a physical education or personal, social and health education programme.	A specific focus can help ensure that HRE does not become lost or take second place to other information. HRE is less likely to be regarded as an assumed 'by-product' of physical education lessons, and HRE is perceived as important through having its own time slot and identity. The value and status of the associated knowledge, understanding and skills are raised.	HRE may be seen in isolation and not closely linked to other areas of physical education. The HRE knowledge, understanding and skills may be delivered over a period of time with long gaps in between, which is problematic in terms of cohesion and progression (e.g. one short block of work per year). The knowledge base may be delivered in such a way as to reduce activity levels within physical education (e.g. too much teacher talk).
Topic An approach involving a series of lessons following a specific topic or theme that is taught through physical education and classroom lessons. This may incorporate both permeation and focused units.	HRE may be delivered in a more holistic manner, with closer links to other health behaviours (such as eating a balanced diet) and other National Curriculum subjects. The area can be covered in more depth and be closely related to pupils' personal experiences. The amount of time engaged in physical activity in physical education lessons might be increased if introductory and follow-up work is conducted in the classroom.	A topic- or theme-based approach may be more time consuming with respect to planning. This approach could be less practically oriented than other approaches (if it incorporates a high degree of classroom-based work).

Combined/mixed	This builds on the strengths of each	Combined approaches initially
Any combination of permeation, focused and topic-based approaches is possible.	approach. It ensures that value is placed on HRE and that the area of work is closely linked to all physical education experiences and other health behaviours and related subjects.	may be more time consuming to plan, structure, implement and co-ordinate within the curriculum.

Adapted, with permission, from J. Harris, 2001, *Health-Related Exercise in the National Curriculum: Key Stages 1 to 4.* (Champaign, IL: Human Kinetics), p. 41.

The most common, and we believe, preferred and effective approach used by schools is likely to be a combination of approaches (i.e. focused units of work in physical education, integration through other areas of physical education and delivery within other areas of the curriculum). As you can see from Table 7.3, this approach builds on the strengths of the others and in our view provides a realistic opportunity to address more adequately the knowledge base associated with the area. It also suggests to us that value is being placed on HRE and that teachers have taken the time to plan, structure, implement and co-ordinate the area. However, yourself and your department, being familiar with your curriculum, staff and students, are in the best position to decide which approach or approaches to adopt, based on your knowledge of the strengths and limitations of each.

Delivery

The misunderstandings and misinterpretations of HRE we identified earlier have perhaps also led to a number of additional undesirable practices concerning the delivery of HRE. We wish to highlight these here as well as a number of desirable practices, and ask you to consider which practices most closely reflect current practices in your department:

HRE	Desirable practices	Undesirable practices
Status	Explicit, valued, planned, evaluated	Implicit, low status, incidental, not monitored
Breadth and relevance	Comprehensive, meaningful, focus on health/activity participation	Narrow, superficial, emphasis on fitness testing/hard training/elite performance
Coherence and status	Coherent, co-ordinated, clear links with other areas of physical education/personal, social and health education and related subjects, integrated	Ad hoc, hit and miss, limited links with other areas of physical education/personal, social and health education and related subjects
Equity	Inclusive, involving all pupils	Exclusive, reduced or minimal involvement of pupils such as the least active, less competent and those with disabilities and health conditions
Action	Requires guidance and support	Requires change

(Adapted from Harris, 2000, p. 17)

The aim of course, is to eradicate the undesirable practices in favour of desirable ones. Yet evidence suggests that many schools may not be achieving the desirable practices. For example, studies conducted in the United Kingdom have found that only approximately a third to a half of schools consider the teaching of HRE in their schools to be fully structured, that many health-related programmes are focused more on 'fitness for sports performance' than 'fitness for healthy lifestyles', and that, rather than promoting equity and inclusion, gendered practices through 'female' and 'male' versions of HRE are common.

The way in which you present HRE information and physical activity experiences to your students is obviously critical. To encourage your students to value and aspire to being physically active (and fit), your HRE (and all physical education!) lessons must involve enjoyable, positive and meaningful exercise experiences, a practical knowledge base and caring teaching strategies.

Finally, in promoting physical activity within the curriculum you need to place emphasis on the beneficial short- and long-term effects of exercise, improved functional capacity, weight management and psychological well-being associated with exercise participation. Warning your students of the risks of inactivity, for example of developing hypokinetic diseases such as coronary heart disease and obesity, and threats of illness and death alone will do very little to switch them on to physical activity. As we noted in Chapter 3, teenagers feel invincible and live in the present, and therefore believe that they are immune from such problems! It is also important that you encourage your students to shift from dependence on yourself as the teacher to independence, by helping them to acquire the understanding, competence and confidence required to be independently active.

References

Department for Education and Employment and Qualifications and Curriculum Authority (1999), *The National Curriculum. Handbook for Secondary Teachers in England*. London: HMSO.

Harris, J. (2000), *Health-Related Exercise in the National Curriculum. Key Stages 1 to 4*. Champaign, IL: Human Kinetics.

Qualifications and Curriculum Authority (2007), *New Secondary Curriculum*. http://curriculum.qca.org.uk

Qualifications and Curriculum Authority (2007), *New Secondary Curriculum. Physical Education Programmes of Study Key Stages 3 and 4*. http://curriculum.qca.org.uk

Introduction

In the previous chapter we looked at how the physical education curriculum, and particularly health-related exercise (HRE), can promote physical activity and we discussed some important developments as well as the interpretation, philosophy, content, organization and delivery of HRE. From this, we hope you'll agree that there is real scope to make a difference through the physical education curriculum. However, despite such developments and opportunities, we feel that many schools are not maximizing the potential of their curriculum. In this chapter, we offer some possible reasons for this, raise some important issues, and make some recommendations to assist you in helping and encouraging your department to realize the potential of your curriculum.

Status and time

The time allocated to physical education in the United Kingdom has been found to be among the lowest in Europe. Physical education is generally seen as a competing subject to the core subjects of mathematics, English and science and, given the pressures of time and the need for good examination results, the physical education curriculum, school sport and physical activity promotion may be viewed as being relatively low priority in some schools. As a result, convincing senior management, other teachers and parents of the status of physical education and securing and/or maintaining adequate curriculum time for the subject may be a challenge.

On a brighter note though, the government, via the Physical Education and Sport Strategy for Young People and associated targets has, and continues to do much to try to secure and increase curriculum time for physical education. As we noted in the previous chapter, the government's long-term ambition for 2010 is to ensure that all children have two hours of curriculum physical education per week. Furthermore, recent surveys such as Sport England's Young People and Sport Survey (2002) and the School Sport Survey (2006/2007) suggest there has been an increase in the number of schools reaching this target.

Yet, even within existing physical education time, physical activity promotion is not often given the time and status it deserves in the physical education curriculum and there is no guarantee that the situation will change even with more time. Despite a stronger positioning of health issues within the curriculum in recent years (e.g. through the National Curriculum for Physical Education (NCPE)), the effect may be small because many physical education teachers prefer and would rather teach competitive sport.

> **Recommendation** – Work to raise the status of physical education and physical activity promotion in your school (see Chapters 10, 11 and 12 for ideas of how to do this). If applicable, lobby headteachers, senior management and governors for more physical education time. Use the information in Chapters 1 and 2 of this book to help you present your argument. If you already have sufficient time, ensure you retain it by using it well.

Teacher knowledge, understanding and attitudes

The concerns we identified in Chapter 7 over the limited systematic expression of health in physical education and the variations in HRE practice have been partly blamed on teachers' lack of knowledge. While teachers generally value and believe in the importance of promoting physical activity among their students, a number, through no fault of their own, have relatively limited knowledge of how to go about doing this. Health or physical activity promotion and especially the recommended teaching methods may be alien to some teachers.

The likely reason is that few physical education teachers have been adequately trained in health-based work and physical activity promotion within their own teacher training. The structure of initial teacher training courses, as well as financial and time constraints, often mean that trainee teachers have limited practical exercise teaching experience. This presents problems for the future development of the area when these new teachers enter the profession. Also, the approach many physical education teachers adopt to the area, which is often overly scientific and 'fitness' oriented, has been criticized and blamed on the highly scientized physical education/sports science courses from which physical education teachers normally graduate. In other words, teachers are simply regurgitating what they themselves were taught at college or university.

The subject knowledge issue needs to be tackled by the profession and within initial teacher training such that teachers feel confident and knowledgeable promoters of health and exercise. The curriculum resource published by Harris (see Chapter 7) was an important and welcomed development in this respect and we are optimistic that it can and has made a difference to teachers' practice. Indeed, the resource was 'kitemarked' by the Teacher Training Agency (now the Training and Development Agency for Schools) in recognition of its significant contribution to developing subject knowledge in physical education and in the hope that it would be used by all initial teacher training providers.

Recommendations – If needed, attend continuing professional development in the area of health and fitness and encourage colleagues to do likewise. Access relevant resources and contacts to assist with the area (see Chapter 13). If applicable, when recruiting new staff, advertise for and look for someone with strengths in the area.

Links to other curriculum areas

Many opportunities exist, and should be grasped, to reinforce health and fitness work in other curriculum areas. Quite simply, the more knowledge, understanding and key messages can be reinforced and supported across subjects the better, as the more successful your efforts are likely to be.

Perhaps the most explicit and more formal links are between personal, social and health education, science and design and technology. As applicable, we have outlined the most obvious links between these subjects and HRE at Key Stages 3 and 4 for you in Tables 8.1 and 8.2.

Table 8.1 HRE within the National Curriculum at Key Stage 3: Physical Education, Personal, Social and Health Education: Personal Well-being, Science and Design and Technology

	Physical Education	PSHE: Personal Wellbeing
Key concepts Involves pupils:	**Healthy, active lifestyles** • understanding that physical activity contributes to the healthy functioning of the body and mind and is an essential component of a healthy lifestyle • recognizing that regular physical activity that is fit for purpose, safe and enjoyable has the greatest impact on physical, mental and social well-being	**Healthy lifestyles** • recognizing that healthy lifestyles, and the wellbeing of self and others, depend on information and making responsible choices • understanding that physical, mental, sexual and emotional health affect our ability to lead fulfilling lives, and that there is help and support available when they are threatened • dealing with growth and change as normal parts of growing up **Risk** • understanding risk in both positive and negative terms and understanding that individuals need to manage risk to themselves and others in a range of situations • developing the confidence to try new ideas and face challenges safely, individually and in groups
Key processes Pupils should be able to:	**Developing physical and mental capacity** • develop their physical strength, stamina, speed and flexibility to cope with the demands of different activities • develop their mental determination to succeed **Making informed choices about healthy, active lifestyles** • identify the types of activity they are best suited to • identify the types of role they would like to take on • make choices about their involvement in healthy physical activity	**Critical reflection** • reflect on personal strengths, achievements and areas for development • identify and use strategies for setting and meeting personal targets in order to increase motivation • develop self-awareness by reflecting critically on their behaviour and its impact on others • use knowledge and understanding to make informed choices about safety, health and wellbeing • find information and support from a variety of sources • assess and manage the element of risk in personal choices and situations

Table 8.1 (Contd)

	Physical Education	PSHE: Personal Wellbeing	Science	Design and Technology
Range and content				
Study should include:	Exercising safely and effectively to improve health and wellbeing, as in fitness and health activities represents one area of six, at least four of which should be covered	• the knowledge and skills needed for setting realistic targets and personal goals • physical and emotional change and puberty • how a balanced diet and making choices for being healthy contribute to personal well-being, and the importance of balance between work, leisure and exercise • ways of recognizing and reducing risk, minimizing harm and getting help in emergency and risky situations • a knowledge of basic first aid	**Organisms, behaviour and health** • life processes are supported by the organization of cells into tissues, organs and body systems • conception, growth, development, behaviour and health can be affected by diet, drugs and disease • behaviour is influenced by internal and external factors and can be investigated and measured	At least one of food or textiles area should be included. **Food** • healthy eating models relating to a balanced diet, the nutritional needs of different groups in society and the factors affecting food choice and how to take these into account when planning, preparing and cooking meals and products • the characteristics of a broad range of ingredients, including their nutritional, functional and sensory properties
	Physical Education	PSHE: Personal Wellbeing		
Curriculum opportunities				
Opportunities for pupils to:	• get involved in a broad range of different activities that, in combination, develop the whole body • follow pathways to other activities in and beyond school	• make real choices and decisions based on accurate information obtained through their own research using a range of sources, including the internet, other media sources and visits/visitors to and from the wider community		

Table 8.2 HRE within the National Curriculum at Key Stage 4: Physical Education, Personal, Social and Health Education: Personal Wellbeing and Science

	Physical Education	PSHE: Personal Wellbeing
Key concepts Involves pupils:	**Healthy, active lifestyles** • understanding that physical activity contributes to the healthy functioning of the body and mind and is an essential component of a healthy lifestyle • recognizing that regular physical activity that is fit for purpose, safe and enjoyable has the greatest impact on physical, mental and social wellbeing	**Healthy lifestyles** • recognizing that healthy lifestyles, and the well-being of self and others, depend on information and making responsible choices • understanding that our physical, mental, sexual and emotional health affect our ability to lead fulfilling lives and that there is help and support available when they are threatened • dealing with growth and change as normal parts of growing up **Risk** • understanding risk in both positive and negative terms and understanding that individuals need to manage risk to themselves and others in a range of personal and social situations • developing the confidence to try new ideas and face challenges safely, individually and in groups
	Physical Education	PSHE: Personal Wellbeing
Key processes Pupils should be able to:	**Developing physical and mental capacity** • analyse how mental and physical capacity affects performance • maintain and develop their physical strength, stamina, speed and flexibility to cope with the demands of different activities and active lifestyles • prepare mentally for successful involvement in physical activity, performance and engagement in healthy, active lifestyles	**Critical reflection** • reflect on their own and others' strengths and achievements; give and receive constructive praise and criticism, and learn from success and failure • identify and use strategies for setting and meeting personal targets and challenges in order to increase motivation, reflect on their effectiveness and implement and monitor strategies for achieving goals • develop self-awareness by reflecting critically on their behaviour and its impact on others

Table 8.2 (Contd)

	Physical Education	PSHE: Personal Well-being
	Making informed choices about healthy, active lifestyles • identify the types of physical activity available to them and the roles they would like to take on • link physical activity with diet, work and rest for personal health and well-being • make informed decisions about getting involved in a lifetime of healthy physical activities that suit their needs	**Decision making and managing risk** • use knowledge and understanding to make informed choices about safety, health and well-being, evaluating personal choices and making changes if necessary • find and evaluate information, advice and support from a variety of sources and be able to support others in doing so • assess and manage risk in personal choices and situations, minimize harm in risky situations and demonstrate how to help others do so

	Physical Education	PSHE: Personal Well-being	Science
Range and content Study should include	Exercising safely and effectively to improve health and well-being, as in fitness and health activities represents one area of six, at least two of which should be covered	• how the media portrays young people, body image and health issues • the characteristics of emotional and mental health, and the causes, symptoms and treatments of some mental and emotional health disorders • the benefits and risks of health and lifestyle choices, including choices relating to sexual activity and substance use and misuse, and the short- and long-term consequences for the health and mental and emotional well-being of individuals, families and communities • where and how to obtain health information, how to recognize and follow health and safety procedures, ways of reducing risk and minimizing harm in risky situations, how to find sources of emergency help and how to use basic and emergency first aid	**Organisms and health*** • the ways in which organisms function are related to the genes in their cells • chemical and electrical signals enable body systems to respond to internal and external changes, in order to maintain the body in an optimal state • human health is affected by a range of environmental and inherited factors, by the use and misuse of drugs and by medical treatments * note – the above represents the 'breadth of study' for Science at Key Stage 4

	Physical Education	PSHE: Personal Wellbeing
Curriculum opportunities Opportunities for pupils to:	• get involved in a broad range of different activities that, in combination, develop the whole body • follow pathways to other activities in and beyond school	• make real choices and decisions based on accurate information obtained through their own research using a range of sources, including national and local/ward data, the internet, other media sources and visits/visitors to or from the wider community

With some thought and mapping though, virtually all curriculum areas can and should contribute to HRE in important ways. We provide just a few examples.

- Geography – mapping, compass work and orienteering; environmental issues around traffic pollution, town planning for physical activity and safety (e.g. for cycling, walking); leisure, sport and recreation in cities, countryside, seaside resorts; local walks to examine urban and recreation planning.
- History – leisure, sport and recreation over the years; history of sport; women in sport.
- IT – using search engines to explore local physical activity and sporting opportunities; compiling and creating a physical activity directory using multimedia; recording and analysing physical activity and physical fitness data; calculating time spent in physical activity, improvements in fitness.
- Languages – the leisure, recreation and sporting habits of the country; physical activity, fitness and sports vocabulary; discussing own physical activity and sporting interests, likes, dislikes.
- Design and Technology – designing and making 'active toys' (e.g. target games, skipping rope, Frisbee, kite, miniature sailing boat); designing activity/sports clothing.
- Art – designing physical activity promotion posters; compiling and creating a physical activity directory; painting 'active' murals around school and playground markings for various games/activities.
- Music – different forms of dance music; music, rhythms and dances from different cultures.

Despite the obvious potential, communication between staff and subjects on the topic of health and fitness is often limited.

> **Recommendation** – Make time for liaison and curriculum mapping (e.g. training days, departmental/faculty or staff meetings). It's good to talk!

Research developments

Over time, and in the last ten years in particular, a number of advancements in research have taken place which have improved our understanding of children's physical fitness, physical activity and health. These developments are exciting and are very much needed, but they further complicate and have implications for your work and efforts to promote physical activity. Below we have highlighted just a few of the important developments you should be aware of.

Physical activity recommendations

An important issue in promoting physical activity relates to what type of and how much physical activity children should do. We addressed and provided ideas for implementing these recommendations in Chapter 4.

> **Recommendation** – In order to give your students appropriate guidance, you should make sure you are aware of the recent physical activity recommendations for young people and their implications for practice, as well as their limitations.

The nature of children's physical activity

Researchers have now begun to provide a more detailed picture of children's physical activity patterns (see Chapter 2) which has implications for the type of activities we make available to young people. Children 'do activity in different ways than adults' and engage in short, brisk bursts of activity, for example, as in 'tag', 'chase' or skipping games. Teenagers' activity tends to be more adult-like and is likely to involve more sustained moderate activity such as that obtained through sports or exercise such as jogging, cycling or aerobic dance.

Another aspect to consider is the settings in which children are usually active. Children can be active in different settings, in a variety of ways, and at particular times of the day, including by:

◆ active transport to and from school (e.g. walking);
◆ informal play during school breaks and lunch times;
◆ informal play after school;
◆ formal sports, physical education and exercise training;
◆ active jobs (for older children).

These categories and settings for physical activity suggest that it may be useful for teachers to consider *activity profiles* with students. The balance between these settings and ways of being active can vary a great deal between individuals or groups of students and activity targets can be set and achieved in very different ways using *profiles*. Profiles would incorporate the activity students do through transport, informal play, sports practice and games, work, and also sedentary time. Thus, two equally active students in terms of overall amount of physical activity might display very different activity patterns or profiles and derive their activity in very different ways. For example one student, Emma, aged 12, might derive her activity from formal sport at school, weekends and during the evenings, whereas another student Phillip, also aged 12, might be active through playing sport on the local recreation ground, walking to school and doing a half-hour paper round each morning.

Using this approach encourages teachers to look beyond the confines of physical education or sport as the answer, to a wider range of possible solutions. It also helps to draw out important gender, age, ethnic and social group differences in children's activity needs.

> **Recommendations** – Become familiar with the physical activity patterns of your students. Introduce your students to activity profiles and use them to set activity targets, taking into account the range of categories and settings and your students' needs.

The determinants of physical activity in children

As we noted in Chapter 3, knowledge of the determinants or correlates of physical activity, or the factors that influence children's physical activity, is important in order that teachers can address these, challenge the barriers and constraints to participation, and explore with students ways of overcoming them.

> **Recommendation** – Familiarize yourself with the factors that affect your students' participation (see Chapter 3) and try to influence these by implementing some of the ideas provided in Chapter 3.

Making physical activity and sport relevant and attractive to children

Physical education time makes a valuable contribution to the physical activity needs of your students, but it cannot satisfy them. You therefore need to carefully consider how physical education can most effectively contribute to promoting healthy, active lifestyles and provide opportunities for all your students to engage in appropriate amounts of physical activity. Schools primarily influence students' leisure time physical activity through the positive physical education and sport experiences and teaching they provide. Of course, the opposite is also true! The content and delivery of your physical education programme, as well as the opportunities beyond the curriculum and school (see Chapter 10), therefore need careful consideration. We discussed the philosophy and delivery of HRE in Chapter 7, and the points and issues we raised are very relevant here. In addition, we feel a few specific issues are worthy of a special mention.

Delivery

The desirable practices and principles for the delivery of HRE we advocated in Chapter 7 should, of course, be adopted and physical activity promotion should be identified as a distinct objective within a structured physical education programme. Two specific yet commonly debated issues concerning delivery which are likely to influence children's experiences and enjoyment of physical education include (i) increasing physical activity levels during physical education lessons, and (ii) fitness testing.

Increasing physical activity levels

Concerns have been expressed over the low level of moderate to vigorous physical activity that children often experience during physical education lessons and the amount of time they spend sitting down, listening, and/or waiting their turn. In their Health Position Paper (of May 2008), the Association for Physical Education (AfPE) recommends that to increase the amount of physical activity in physical education lessons pupils should be actively moving for at least 50 per cent of the available learning time.

The desire to increase activity levels within physical education does however need to be approached sensibly, otherwise it may prompt some inappropriate responses. Appropriate responses include careful attention to planning and organization (e.g. tasks set, grouping procedures, organization of equipment and resources, modification of tasks/rules or games) to maximize activity time. Inevitably there will still be time when students are inactive, but when not physically active they should be involved in tasks which develop their knowledge and understanding (e.g. listening to succinct explanations, observing relevant demonstrations, answering focused questions) and which enhance their planning and evaluating skills (e.g. making decisions about how to link movements within a sequence).

Also the assessment of students' knowledge and understanding should be through practically applied tasks in which they are active (e.g. performing part of a warm up), rather than sitting down written tests. Some non-active tasks (e.g. finding out about activity opportunities in the local community) could be incorporated within related curriculum areas (e.g. PSHE). We feel that the above are not only desirable in terms of promoting health benefits and student involvement, but are also likely to be more enjoyable for students.

Inappropriate responses to increasing children's activity levels in lessons include teachers adopting a hard-line approach and forcing students into 'tough' exercise, such as arduous cross-country running, fitness regimes involving dull, boring and repetitive drill-type activities, or fitness testing. We feel that these practices are not only guaranteed to turn most youngsters off rather than on to physical education, sport and physical activity for life but, as we have noted in earlier chapters, they may be at the expense of developing knowledge and understanding about physical activity, and the physical and behavioural skills students need so as to engage in a physically active lifestyle.

Fitness testing
We have already looked at the issue of fitness testing in Chapter 5. All we wish to say or reiterate here is that, from a curriculum point of view, a concern about fitness testing in physical education lessons is the amount of time often spent on it without necessarily positively influencing students' fitness or activity levels or their attitudes towards physical activity. As we noted in Chapter 5, testing can be counterproductive in that it can be demeaning, embarrassing and uncomfortable for some children, often those about whom there is most concern (e.g. the least fit/active, the overweight), and reinforces the idea that exercise is competitive and unpleasant.

Content
The physical education profession and the government have been accused of viewing sport, and especially team games, as the primary

focus of physical education and the main vehicle for promoting healthy, active lifestyles. Despite subsequent revisions of the NCPE and the removal of the statutory requirement to teach games, initially at Key Stage 4 within Curriculum 2000, and more recently at Key Stages 3 and 4 (QCA, 2007), competitive sports and team games which focus on performance have, and it is felt will continue to, dominate the physical education curriculum. Even some of the NCPE terminology, which refers to 'developing physical and mental capacity' and 'fitness activities' illustrates the continued and important influence of and focus on sport and performance in physical education.

But, we need to consider how relevant and appealing competitive sports and team games are to many youngsters. For example, these do not reflect the types of physical activity children choose to engage in during their leisure time when they have 'free' choice. As Chapter 2 revealed, when given the choice many children today are opting to take part in more lifestyle, non-competitive and recreational activities or sporting forms such as walking, cycling and swimming rather than competitive and performance-based sports. If the physical education profession ignores this and persistently pushes traditional physical education, many more children may be switched off physical activity.

On a more positive note, we are aware that many schools and teachers have begun to respond to the changing lifestyles and physical activity interests of their students and are now supplementing the traditional physical education curriculum with a much broader range of activities which better meet their students' needs. If teachers are serious about influencing children's physical activity, then these efforts need to continue. Furthermore, the new Secondary NCPE provides more flexibility and scope for schools to do this. For example, it is encouraging to see a move away from the six activity areas of previous National Curricula within the 'range and content' and mention of a much broader range of activities which physical education teachers might draw on. Examples include Gaelic football, water polo, fencing, judo, synchronized swimming, street or ballroom dancing, skateboarding, golf, archery, orienteering, aqua aerobics, weight training and power walking, to name but a few.

To address the changing lifestyles and physical activity interests of your students, we suggest you think about:

◆   introducing more individual sports (e.g. racket, orienteering) and individualized fitness activities (e.g. aerobics, circuits, swimming for fitness);

- providing activities acceptable to a range of adolescent subcultures (e.g. aerobics, step or aquafit may be more acceptable to girls than hockey or netball);
- teaching the 'why' of physical activity in the curriculum;
- helping students develop self-management skills that equip them to make lifestyle changes;
- creating a teaching or coaching climate where students can develop a sense of responsibility.

We have included many more examples and ideas of activities and initiatives you could introduce in the following chapters.

Time for reflection

Finally, we encourage you to reflect on the following questions. Where possible, also discuss them with and seek the views of colleagues and your students.

- What is your experience of physical education and physical activity promotion in your school and other schools with which you are familiar?
- Based on your experiences in your own school, do you feel the issues and concerns we have highlighted in this chapter are justified? In particular:
  - Is physical education and physical activity promotion given adequate status and time?
  - Are teachers (including yourself) knowledgeable and positive about physical activity promotion?
  - How can you, and your colleagues, keep up to date with relevant research and developments?
  - Is the physical education programme (content) relevant and attractive for all students?
  - Is the physical education programme delivered in a way that is conducive to promoting physical activity to all students?

References

The Association for Physical Education. (May 2008), *Health Position Paper*.

Sport England (2003), *Young People and Sport in England. Trends in Participation 1994–2002*. London: Sport England.

TNS Social Research (2007), *2006/07 School Sport Survey*. London: TNS UK Limited.

Physical activity, physical education and childhood obesity

Introduction

We are bombarded almost daily with government, scientific or media reports and messages concerning the growing problem of obesity and the possible consequences of this on the population's health. Indeed, it has been alleged that an obesity epidemic is sweeping our nation. What is more, the problem also extends to children, an increasing number of whom are now reported to be obese. This has led to various policies, strategies and responses from government as well as from individual schools and teachers themselves who are feeling compelled and even duty bound to act and address the problem. However, we, and others, feel that some of the reports and messages, and more worrying still, some of the measures being taken or advocated to tackle the issue are misleading or misguided and could do more harm than good.

For the above reason, we have chosen to focus this chapter on physical activity, physical education and childhood obesity and to consider the role that physical education and you as a teacher can potentially and sensibly play in addressing childhood obesity. To begin with and to set the context, we present some general background information concerning childhood obesity and identify some of the key issues, considerations and sensitivities. We then look at some of the formal guidance and recommendations that are available, before offering some practical recommendations for promoting physical activity with obese youngsters.

Definitions, facts and figures

Obesity is a recognized clinical health condition. A commonly accepted way of measuring obesity is to use the Body Mass Index (BMI). This is determined by an individual's weight (kg) divided by their height squared (m^2). The World Health Organization guidelines define individuals with a BMI of 25kg/m^2 or more as overweight, and those with a BMI of 30 kg/m^2 as obese. However, there are limitations of using BMI as a measure of obesity as, because it is based on weight and height, it does not discriminate between fat and fat-free (or lean) mass, which can lead to the misclassification of some individuals. For example, some individuals may be classified as overweight or even obese when in reality they are muscular and well toned.

Measurement issues aside, a number of studies conducted in the United Kingdom in recent years have reported an increased prevalence of obesity in children. The extent of this, however, is open to debate and studies have reported conflicting figures which have often been interpreted in different ways and raised varying levels of alarm. A possible reason for this is that the figures for overweightness are often included with or cited alongside the obesity figures. Failure to make the distinction between the two in this way is problematic in that it artificially inflates the statistics and therefore confuses and distorts the picture. Also, and as just noted, obesity is a clinical health condition whereas overweightness is not and, whilst the latter can lead to the former, it may not necessarily.

To give some broad figures however, the Health Survey for England 2006 revealed around three in ten boys and girls aged 2 to 15 years to be either overweight or obese (31 per cent and 29 per cent respectively), and noted a rise in obesity levels between 1995–2006 in both sexes (from 11 per cent to 17 per cent for boys and from 12 per cent to 15 per cent for girls). Furthermore, some experts have estimated that these figures will continue to rise and that two thirds of children will be overweight or obese and a quarter will be obese by 2050. Others, however, refute such findings and predictions, claiming that they are exaggerated, sensationalized, and even misreported, especially where the overweight and obesity figures have been combined. Although the above might seem somewhat confusing, what nevertheless can be deduced is that the general trend of childhood obesity is upwards. Thus, an increasing number of students in your classes will be overweight and/or obese.

Associated health problems

There are concerns about the impact of childhood obesity on children's current physical and mental health. Yet, while the physical health consequences of obesity in adults are reasonably well known and include, for example, increased incidence of hypertension, type 2 diabetes, abnormal blood lipid (fat) levels, and increased risk of certain cancers, the impact of obesity on children's health is less clear. Nonetheless, studies indicate that obese children have an increased risk of cardiovascular disease risk factors (e.g. hypertension, adverse blood lipid profile) and of developing type 2 diabetes, a condition that was once typically only associated with adults.

Obesity in childhood can also lead to other complications or problems of both a physical and psychological nature. Examples of physical complications include respiratory problems such as asthma, poor exercise tolerance and sleep apnoea (a disturbance to one's breathing during sleep), and orthopaedic problems such as poor posture, back pain, ankle sprains, 'knock' knees, flat feet and fractures. Psychological problems include social isolation and discrimination, low self-esteem, depression, learning difficulties and body dissatisfaction or body image disorder.

Finally, and perhaps the most significant health risk faced by obese children, is that they are much more likely to become obese adults and therefore encounter health problems in adulthood. For example, long-term health consequences of obesity include increased risk of cardiovascular disease, diabetes and some cancers.

Factors contributing to obesity

Genetics can make some children more susceptible to becoming obese than others, but this alone is not sufficient to cause obesity. Obesity and the increase in obesity is more likely a result of behavioural (i.e. changes in physical activity, diet and eating patterns) and environmental factors (e.g. access to physical activity opportunities, increased availability and affordability of certain types of food).

Quite simply, individuals gain excess weight when energy intake (what we eat and drink; calories consumed) exceeds energy expenditure (what we expend in daily life and through physical activity; calories burned). The energy balance equation explains the relationship between energy intake and energy expenditure:

Energy intake $=$ energy expenditure $\rightarrow$ weight is stable
Energy intake $>$ energy expenditure $\rightarrow$ weight is gained
Energy intake $<$ energy expenditure $\rightarrow$ weight is lost

As we revealed in Chapter 2, although it cannot be firmly established whether children's physical activity has decreased over the years, there is some indirect evidence to suggest this. Furthermore, children's lifestyle and travel patterns have changed with youngsters spending more time in sedentary pursuits and fewer walking or cycling to school, leaving less time or providing fewer opportunities for physical activity. Indeed, some studies have shown a positive relationship between childhood overweightness and time spent watching television, therefore illustrating the importance of lifestyle and physical activity in weight management. Parental physical activity has also been identified as a strong (but not sole) determinant of childhood obesity.

In addition, evidence from national (e.g. the National Diet and Nutrition Survey (2000) and other surveys show that a high proportion of children aged 7 to 14 do not meet national recommended guidelines for healthy eating and that today's youth are consuming too much sugar and fat, and not enough fruit and vegetables. One possible reason is that we now snack, eat out and rely on convenience and fast food more than ever before. These foods tend to be very energy dense (i.e. they contain a lot of calories in relation to their size), and the high consumption of these is recognized to be a cause of obesity. Another reason is likely to be increased portion sizes with 'king size' chocolate bars, 'go large' fast food meals and 'triple pack' sandwiches now being readily available. Although cost-wise these might be better value compared to standard-size portions, they can very easily and substantially increase the calories consumed.

The importance of physical activity and physical activity promotion to obese children

Throughout this book, the importance of promoting physical activity to *all* children has been highlighted for a number of reasons. For obese youngsters though, the promotion of physical activity may be even more crucial and significant. The benefits of physical activity were highlighted in Chapter 1 but some of these are particularly relevant to obese children. For example, physical activity can increase lean body mass and energy expenditure, and thereby help in the achievement and maintenance of energy balance and the prevention of further weight gain, and it can improve a child's metabolic profile (e.g. result in favourable changes in blood cholesterol levels and increase insulin sensitivity) and their psychological well-being.

In addition, and as we noted earlier, because obese children may have physical complications such as asthma and poor exercise tolerance, this makes participating in physical activity even more difficult and the child even more prone to being inactive, and to choosing instead to spend their time in sedentary pursuits. Thus, a downward spiral of inactivity can and often does occur. Positive steps to try to prevent this are therefore needed.

Furthermore, there is some evidence to support the effectiveness of physical activity programmes and/or interventions in the prevention of childhood obesity. For example, aerobic exercise prescriptions, reduced television viewing, physical education and other school-based programmes that combine the promotion of a healthy diet and physical activity have been found to be effective in managing children's weight.

Promoting physical activity to obese children

Clearly then, there are important reasons and potential gains to engaging obese children in physical activity and it is important to try to effectively involve such students in the physical activity opportunities you provide both within and beyond school and physical education lessons. In so doing, the same general messages and advice with regards to promoting physical activity to *all* children apply to obese children. Additionally though, there are some specific considerations and sensitivities to be aware of and take into account. Furthermore, although earlier we were critical of the failure to make the distinction between overweight and obese children, in the context of physical activity promotion, it should be realized that a number of the considerations and sensitivities may in fact also apply to overweight youngsters too.

Considerations and sensitivities

Philosophical

As noted in the introduction to this chapter, we along with others feel that some of the measures being taken or advocated to tackle childhood obesity are misguided and could do more harm than good. For example, in 2004 the government set an obesity target which seeks by 2010 to halt the year on rise in obesity among children under the age of 11 through school actions including the measurement of children's BMI.

Primary school children are now weighed and measured in Reception (aged 4 years) and Year 6 (aged 10) using the BMI, and their parents alerted if they are obese. Other measures and efforts schools have been reported to be taking to try to manage the obesity problem include inspecting children's lunch boxes, fingerprint monitoring, introducing health report cards, as well as organizing and delivering fitness testing and 'fat' clubs specifically aimed at overweight or obese students. Such responses represent an overly simplistic and narrow view of obesity and health and of the role schools and physical education can and should play in addressing both. The assumptions being made and the messages being promoted here would seem to be that thin = healthy and good, whereas fat = unhealthy and bad. In our view, reducing health (and physical education) to only the most obvious and easily measured aspects of performance (e.g. weight, height) while promoting these kinds of messages is insensitive and inappropriate and should itself carry a health warning.

On the issue of weighing and measuring children's BMI specifically, it is not necessary to measure obese, or indeed any children for that matter, to tell them something that they already know, and more importantly, no child needs to be measured to be helped to enjoy being physically active. Indeed, overemphasizing 'fat' measurements, may simply contribute a mental health problem to a physical health issue. For example, an obsession with the issue could lead to rising levels of body disaffection among young people (especially girls), the development of harmful relationships with physical activity and food, and even to serious eating disorders. The latter in particular are serious and growing problems in the UK (the combined total for people diagnosed and undiagnosed with an eating disorder is over one million) and adolescence is a high risk period for the development of such disorders.

Practical

Most children who are obese will know their own capabilities and limitations where participating in physical activity is concerned. However, there are some important practical considerations and sensitivities which are likely to affect obese children's ability to perform physical activity as well as their enjoyment and attitude towards it. These clearly have implications for practice in terms of the types of physical activities and experiences offered to ensure that all such students can engage in, and achieve, through safe, effective and enjoyable physical activity. Of course, it is also important to recognize that obese children are not a homogenous group and therefore the physical and psychological characteristics of each individual (e.g. degree of obesity, level of fitness, extent of any other physical limitations, self-esteem, physical activity likes/dislikes and preferences) also need to be considered when promoting physical activity.

Orthopaedic problems – As noted earlier, obese children may have orthopaedic problems such as poor posture, back pain, 'knock' knees and flat feet and are more susceptible to injuries such as fractures. As a result, high impact and explosive activities, because they put a lot of strain on the bones and joints, can cause discomfort for obese children and increase the risk of injury.

Exercise tolerance – Also noted earlier, was how obese children may have particularly poor tolerance for exercise. This is because they tend to have lower fitness levels, and most notably cardiovascular fitness, than children of a normal weight for their age, and are more prone to overheating during exercise. The latter results from their increased body fat which provides more insulation, especially around the core abdominal region. Collectively, this means they are likely to find high intensity and continuous aerobic activities, such as running and jumping, difficult and uncomfortable.

Movement efficiency and body management – Obese children may be less movement efficient in certain activities such as running and cycling as a result of their larger body and greater body weight. They are also likely to struggle managing their body weight and find activities that require carrying or lifting their body, such as running, jumping and taking weight on hands difficult. Equally though, some obese children are often quite skilled, especially in techniques involving small muscle groups, or often have considerable muscular strength and may therefore excel in certain forms of physical activity and athletic events.

Self-esteem/confidence and self-consciousness/embarrassment – Lack of self-esteem/confidence can often lead to self-consciousness/embarrassment and, in particular, obese children are likely to feel very sensitive and uncomfortable about displaying their bodies in front of others. Changing, showering and physical activities which are particularly public in nature (e.g. athletics races, dance and gymnastic displays) may therefore present particular stresses and challenges for obese youngsters.

Isolation and non participation – The social isolation and discrimination obese children may face as a result of their different body shape means they can easily become non-participants in physical activity and physical education as they do not readily feel accepted as co-participants by their peers. This is likely to be more of an issue in competitive situations.

Guidance and recommendations

Despite the above, there is no reason why most children who are obese should not participate in physical activity or take part in regular physical education lessons. Indeed, the importance and particular benefits of doing so were noted earlier. In this respect, formal guidance has been produced and recommendations made on overweight and/or obesity by key organizations such as the British Heart Foundation, the National Institute for Health and Clinical Excellence and the Department of Health, a brief summary of which are presented below. Following are some 'common sense' recommendations aimed specifically for you as a physical education teacher. In addition, the issues, implications and recommendations for promoting physical activity outlined in Chapter 3 with regards to 'what switches children on and off?' physical activity (see Table 3.2) equally apply, and ideally should be read in conjunction with the guidance and recommendations here.

British Heart Foundation guidance

The British Heart Foundation (1999) suggests that overweight and obese children and young people should focus on three targets which relate to influencing their energy expenditure:

1. Engaging in more weight-bearing activity as part of the daily routine, e.g. walking, climbing stairs.
2. Spending less time in sedentary pursuits such as watching television, reading and listening to music.
3. Performing longer bouts of exercise which are sustained for 40 minutes or more.

National Institute for Clinical Excellence (NICE) guidance

NICE published guidance on the prevention and management of obesity in adults and children in 2006 which includes guidance for schools. NICE recommends that headteachers and chairs of governors, in collaboration with parents and pupils, should assess the whole-school environment and ensure that the ethos of all school policies helps children and young people to maintain a healthy weight, eat a healthy diet and be physically active. A summary of the specific targets and actions suggested by NICE are outlined in Table 9.1.

Table 9.1 NICE obesity guidance for schools

School policies and school environment

Ensure school policies and the school's environment encourages physical activity and a healthy diet. Consider:

◆ Building layout
◆ Provision of recreational spaces
◆ Catering, including vending machines
◆ Food brought into school by the children
◆ The curriculum, including physical education
◆ School travel plans, including provision for cycling
◆ Extended schools.

Staff training

Teaching, support and catering staff should have training on how to implement healthy school policies.

Links with relevant organizations and professionals

Establish links with health professionals and those involved in local strategies and partnerships to promote sports for children and young people.

Interventions

◆ Introduce sustained interventions to encourage pupils to develop lifelong healthy habits.
◆ Take pupils' views into account, and barriers such as cost or concerns about the taste of healthy food.
◆ Physical education staff should promote activities that children enjoy and can take part in outside school and continue into adulthood.
◆ Children should eat meals in a pleasant sociable environment free from distractions.
◆ Involve parents where possible, for example, through special events, newsletters and information about lunch menus.

Adapted from NICE (2006). *Obesity: Guidance on the prevention, identification, assessment and management of overweight and obesity in adults and children.* Reference guide for local authorities, schools and early years providers, workplaces and the public, p. 9.

Department of Health obesity guidance

In 2007, and using the NICE guidance along with other sources of good practice, the Department of Health published obesity guidance for healthy schools co-ordinators and their partners. The guidance identifies five specific areas on which to concentrate efforts:

1. Ensuring that language and core messages are appropriate
    For example, stressing the importance of a balanced diet rather than 'good' foods and 'bad' foods; that a healthy diet and physical activity is important; that physical activity is not only about sport; stressing the positive, e.g. 'be healthy', 'get active', 'feel better'.
2. Achieving healthy school status
    As the core first step in obesity prevention; adopting a whole-school approach that recognizes all four themes (healthy eating, physical activity, emotional health and well-being and personal social and health education).
3. Ensuring universal prevention
    For example, adopting a school food policy; offering an engaging physical education curriculum and a wide variety of extracurricular activities; developing opportunities for building physical literacy and personal safety skills (e.g. pedestrian safety, cycling).
4. Engaging parents/carers
    For example, engaging parents/carers in changes to school food; encouraging them to make changes at home; helping families understand about healthy eating and physical activity; encouraging parents/carers to be involved in physical activities with their children; arranging activities for parents/carers and their children to do together (e.g. vegetable growing clubs, cooking clubs, sports afternoons); organizing family events.
5. Exploring additional opportunities for the obese/overweight
    Involving external providers (but only those whose work is in line with the principles and processes of the Healthy Schools Programme) in obesity, nutrition and/or physical activity interventions.

General and activity recommendations

The following recommendations (see Table 9.2) take into account the considerations and sensitivities outlined earlier and, as applicable, draw on the formal guidance as well as recommendations which emanated from a specialist seminar on 'Physical Education and Childhood Obesity' organized by the Association for Physical Education (afPE) in 2007. It is hoped that they will help you to respond to obesity and any associated issues appropriately, promote appropriate messages, and effectively promote and involve obese students in physical activity both within and beyond school.

Table 9.2 Recommendations for physical education teachers for addressing childhood obesity

General recommendations	Activity recommendations
Adopt a critical attitude towards what you hear and read about obesity, weight, diet and exercise, and encourage your students to do likewise. Remember that much of the research is conflicting and there is plenty of uncertainty surrounding the issues.	Consider kit/clothing and changing/showering policies and procedures. Be sensitive as to how obese children are likely to feel about what they wear and undressing in front of others, and be flexible and accommodating where possible. For example, try to provide private changing facilities and allow children to wear tracksuit bottoms and, for swimming, T-shirts.
Avoid sensationalizing 'obesity' or 'weight' and adopt a sensitive, caring approach in which you focus on inclusion and learning through physical activity to try to enable all students to engage, enjoy and achieve within the physical activity and physical education context.	Encourage obese students to adopt and maintain regular physical activity, including participation in physical education, even if weight loss is slow or does not occur. They will still derive physical and mental health benefits from the activity.

Where possible, frequently change and vary the choice of activity/activities for obese students (and encourage them to do likewise if exercising on their own), to avoid overuse or fatigue of the same muscle groups and joints. |
| Avoid focusing on 'weight' as a problem. Outside of the extremes, people can be healthy at any weight if they engage in moderate amounts of physical activity and have a healthy diet. Adopt the view, health at any size, and the message that 'it is better (and healthier) to be in shape than to be nicely shaped'. | Adopt aerobic activity as the principal type of activity which involves working the large muscle groups for a sustained period of time. In so doing, keep the activity of a low to moderate intensity (and recognize that it may need to be of a very low level initially). Place emphasis on increasing the duration and frequency of the activity rather than the intensity. Low-impact activities (e.g. walking, stepping) are also likely to be more appropriate as these will reduce stress on the bones and joints and be easier and/or more comfortable. |
| Help all students, regardless of their size or weight, to feel good about their bodies in order to build their competence, confidence and sense of | Encourage obese students to engage in non-weight bearing activities (e.g. swimming, aqua aerobics, seated aerobics, seated multi-gym work, cycling, indoor rowing). These are considered particularly appropriate as the body weight is supported, thereby also reducing stress on the bones and joints and making movement easier and/or more comfortable. |

Table 9.2 (Contd)

General recommendations	Activity recommendations
control. Promote the message 'learn to like your body' and help them to see the body not as the enemy but as part of the whole person.	Incorporate physical activities which will promote and improve muscular strength and endurance. These are important to enable obese children to carry out everyday tasks more easily, which may in turn facilitate a more active lifestyle. Circuits or resistance exercise can be beneficial for this and can also help to increase fat free mass and improve muscle tone.
Physically educate your students about their bodies. Help them to understand that bodies change and are not fixed (i.e. as during puberty). Also help them to understand how the body responds to friendly treatment (i.e. the benefits of physical activity and a healthy diet).	If using fixed resistance equipment, however, intense or maximal resistance work must be avoided. Consult the Guidelines on Health-Related Exercise within Safe Practice in Physical Education (see References) for specific guidelines on resistance training.
	Try to incorporate physical activities which will promote and improve balance and posture. This might be through dance or gymnastic activities, or through circuits or resistance exercise (e.g. the flamingo balance or working the postural muscles such as the shoulders
Help obese children to learn to understand and deal with their individuality, strengths and weaknesses and to be proud of who they are and what they have. Promote the message 'celebrate being social'.	(trapezius/rhomboids) and back (erector spinae) as in 'shoulder squeezes' and 'back lifts'). Games are suitable for most obese children as they typically involve intermittent or short bouts of physical activity, with rest periods. Ensure games and team games especially are managed sensitively though to ensure children are appropriately included and accepted within the group (see following points).
Provide your students with specific guidance about the importance of physical activity, its contribution to healthy weight management, and how to go about becoming more active.	Where appropriate, make adjustments to the size of the activity area, team size or equipment used so as to cater for an individual's body size and/or poor exercise tolerance or movement efficiency. For example, reduce the size of the court/pitch, increase the number of players, use different weight/sized equipment.
Identify students with low activity levels and provide them with personalized guidance and	Select physical activities, tasks, as well as the positions and responsibilities you allocate to

encouragement to achieve manageable physical activity targets (see Chapter 4 for physical activity recommendations and guidance and ideas for applying these in practice).

Encourage your department and physical education colleagues to work alongside other subject staff (e.g. those from personal, social and health education, science, food technology) to ensure that consistent messages are promoted about the contribution of physical activity to healthy weight management.

students carefully and sensitively to avoid obese children becoming disheartened or embarrassed. For example, avoid assault courses which involve children squeezing through or jumping over equipment, unfair races, public displays or activities/games which require constant running or jumping. Also avoid always allocating inactive and/or lower status roles or positions to the obese student(s) in the class (e.g. scorer, goalkeeper, equipment helper).

Consider grouping procedures carefully (e.g. avoid letting students pick teams), and take weight and size into account when grouping students for specific tasks and activities with a partner or within a group/team (e.g. marking/defending or tackling in games, supporting or partner/group balancing in gymnastics).

Beyond the structured and organized physical activity you promote, encourage your students to participate in lifestyle activities such as walking or cycling to school and/or the shops, using the stairs instead of the lift, and assisting with household chores around the home such as cleaning the car and gardening. All of these will increase total energy expenditure. At the same time, encourage them to try to reduce the time they spend in sedentary activities, such as watching television or playing computer or video games.

References

Association for Physical Education (2008), *Safe Practice in Physical Education*. Leeds: Coachwise.

British Heart Foundation (1999), *Obesity: The Report of the BNF Task Force*. London: Blackwell.

Craig, R. and Mindell, J. (2007), *Health Survey 2006. Volume 2. Obesity and Other Risk Factors in Children*. The Information Centre.

Gregory, J. and Lowe, S. (2000), *National Diet and Nutrition Survey: Young People Aged 4 to 18 Years*. London: The Stationery Office.

National Institute for Clinical Excellence Guidance (NICE) (2006), *Obesity: Guidance on the Prevention, Identification, Assessment and Management of Overweight and Obesity in Adults and Children*. Reference Guide for Local Authorities, Schools and Early Years Providers, Workplaces and the Public. London: NICE, p. 9.

IV | How? The Whole School

10 | Whole-school approaches

Introduction

The previous three chapters have highlighted the important role of the physical education curriculum in promoting physical activity. However, when trying to promote healthy, active lifestyles among children, physical education can only provide part of the solution. For example, it constitutes only approximately two per cent of children's waking time and therefore on its own cannot address any shortfalls in their physical activity. Within the curriculum, teachers usually use educational or behavioural approaches which involve presenting persuasive arguments to encourage physical activity along with relevant information to students about the barriers and constraints to their participation. They may also involve students in learning self-management and regulatory skills such as goal setting, programme planning, self-reinforcement and monitoring or time management to encourage their participation. These are important skills for students to acquire if we wish them to become independent, confident, active citizens. But, these approaches are limited as efforts on their own because they target only the individual, tend to be 'victim blaming' – in other words, they hold the student responsible for their physical activity behaviour, and they do not acknowledge other factors which influence their physical activity (e.g. parental support, cost, access to facilities) (see Chapter 3). Within curriculum time, you can and should inform, raise awareness and develop behavioural skills in your students, but you will be relatively powerless in terms of being able to tackle the wider issues associated with their physical activity and lifestyles.

Although we believe that the curriculum is a vitally important avenue for promoting physical activity, we also recognize that it is just one of many aspects of a school that influences children. To increase your chances of positively influencing your students' activity, we feel that the potential of every aspect or the 'whole' school to promote healthy, active lifestyles needs to be explored. In this chapter we take a look at examples of whole-school approaches, including the Healthy School and the Active School, and the potential for you and your school to promote physical activity beyond the curriculum.

Whole-school approaches

In Chapter 3 we identified environmental factors as an important set of correlates of physical activity. In schools, many aspects of the school environment can either promote or inhibit the adoption of a healthy, active lifestyle, and knowledge and understanding gained within the curriculum (see Chapters 7 and 8) can either be reinforced and supported or completely undermined by the wider environment or what we sometimes call the 'hidden curriculum'. For example, a school with poorly maintained playgrounds or playing fields, and 'no ball game' policies at break times and lunch times would suggest to us that it does not value physical activity. There is much that you and your school can and should do beyond the curriculum to demonstrate a commitment to promoting healthy, active lifestyles in your students. This involves exploring the potential of every aspect of your school.

There are a number of good reasons for becoming a Healthy and/or Active School. A Healthy and/or Active School.

- ◆ fosters positive attitudes to health and physical activity among staff and students;
- ◆ puts health and physical activity formally on the school agenda;
- ◆ provides a good marketing tool for the school;
- ◆ reinforces health and/or activity knowledge, understanding and behaviour throughout the whole school and is therefore likely to be more effective;
- ◆ avoids 'victim blaming' (i.e. holding the individual responsible for their physical activity behaviour, as well as ignoring other factors which have an influence);
- ◆ shares the responsibility of promoting health and well-being;
- ◆ encourages working in partnership (e.g. with other schools, external agencies).

The Healthy School

A Healthy School aims to achieve healthy lifestyles for the entire school population including students, staff, governors and parents by developing a supportive environment conducive to the promotion of health. Traditionally, three key elements have formed the basis of a Healthy School:

◆ the curriculum;
◆ the environment (or hidden curriculum);
◆ the community.

The government has supported the idea of Healthy Schools for some time and in 1998 officially launched the National Healthy Schools Programme (NHSP). The government's target is that, by 2009, all schools will be participating in the National Healthy Schools Programme and that 75 per cent will have achieved National Healthy School Status.

The Programme is a joint Department of Health and Department for Children, Schools and Families initiative, the vision of which is for all children and young people to be healthy and achieve at school and in life. The specific aims of the NHSP are:

◆ to support children and young people in developing healthy behaviours;
◆ to help raise achievement;
◆ to help reduce health inequalities;
◆ to help promote social inclusion.

The programme is based on a whole-school approach to physical and emotional well-being which involves working with children and young people, parents, school staff and the whole school community. Such an approach recognizes that being healthy is not just about children and young people and the school curriculum, but about the whole school community and the entire school day.

The NHSP has four themes:

◆ Personal, Social and Health Education (PSHE);
◆ Healthy Eating;
◆ Physical Activity;
◆ Emotional Health and Well-Being.

Each theme includes a number of criteria that schools need to fulfil, using a whole-school approach, in order to achieve National Healthy Schools Status. For example, there are ten criteria for physical activity, which are set out below.

♦ Provides clear leadership and management to develop and monitor its physical activity policy.

♦ Has a whole-school physical activity policy – developed through wide consultation, implemented, monitored and evaluated for impact.

♦ Ensures a minimum of two hours of structured physical activity each week to all of its children and young people in or outside the school curriculum.

♦ Provides opportunities for all children and young people to participate in a broad range of extracurricular activities that promote physical activity.

♦ Consults with children and young people about the physical activity opportunities offered by the school, identifies barriers to participation and seeks to remove them.

♦ Involves School Sport Co-ordinators (where available) and other community resources in the provision of activities.

♦ Encourages children and young people, parents/carers and staff to walk or cycle to school under safer conditions, utilizing the School Travel Plan.*

♦ Gives parents/carers the opportunity to be involved in the planning and delivery of physical activity opportunities and helps them to understand the benefits of physical activity for themselves and their children.

♦ Ensures that there is appropriate training provided for those involved in providing physical activities.

♦ Encourages all staff to undertake physical activity.

* A School Travel Plan is a document which outlines a school's strategy on travel to and from school. A quality plan will include a package of measures to improve road-user safety and reduce car use. The government target is for all schools to have a Travel Plan by 2010.

Local programmes, grounded in local education and health partnerships, support schools in the process of achieving National Healthy School Status. Each Local Authority in England has a Local Healthy Schools Programme which, via a Regional Co-ordinator, offers support to schools. Details of your Local Programme Co-ordinator and more information about the NHSP can be found on the NHSP website: www.healthyschools.gov.uk

Further support specific to physical activity provision and the NHSP physical activity criteria is available in the form of Physical Activity Guidance booklets (see References) which have been developed with the support of the British Heart Foundation and the Association for Physical Education. The purpose of the guidance is to offer support to schools working towards achieving Healthy School Status and demonstrate how physical activity can be promoted throughout the school day and beyond. The booklets have been designed to be used with the NHSP website. They contain advice, materials and practical ideas for schools and provide links to other resources, programmes and templates.

The Active School

The concept of an 'Active School' is not new. Surprisingly though, limited attention has been paid to the notion. An Active School aims to maximize opportunities for children (and all who are associated with the school) to be active by exploring all opportunities and avenues to promote physical activity. The same elements of the curriculum, environment and the community that traditionally have formed the basis of a Healthy School are also important in an Active School.

There is no prescribed or definitive way of becoming an Active School, but as a starting point we recommend that your school develops a Physical Activity or Active School Policy and forms an 'Active School Committee'. Our reasons for recommending such action are:

◆ to ensure that activity promotion is given the status it deserves and is placed on and remains on your school agenda;
◆ to develop a clear vision (goal/objectives) and means (strategies) for increasing participation in physical activity;
◆ to drive, co-ordinate and evaluate physical activity initiatives in your school.

Another option might be for your school to incorporate physical activity objectives and the elements of an Active School Policy into other existing school policies.

An example Active School Policy is shown in Table 10.1, which provides a range of Active School ideas or strategies. We also include many more Active School ideas or physical activity promotion strategies in the next chapter, which are grouped into the broad categories of: school and departmental policies and practices; the physical education programme (curricular and out-of-school hours); school ethos and environment; and community links and partnerships.

Of course every school is different and the content of any policy should be based on the needs and issues of your students and the school, as well as on what is realistic, feasible and practical. We advise you to use the Active School framework and ideas, along with those in the following chapter, as a stimulus for action and to help you to prioritize, plan, select and guide projects and initiatives which are likely to be realistic and manageable.

Table 10.1 Example Active School Policy

Policy aim: To increase physical activity participation across the whole school community by developing a supportive environment conducive to the promotion of physical activity.

Curriculum

* Allocate at least two hours of curriculum time for physical education each week for all students.

* Provide a broad, balanced, relevant and quality physical education programme which complies with statutory requirements and is accessible to and meets the needs and interests of all students.

* Fully implement National Curriculum requirements for HRE through a well structured, planned, delivered and evaluated programme of study.

* Promote physical activity across the curriculum (e.g. mapping in geography, environmental education including traffic pollution, town planning for activity and safety, nature walks in science, measurement in maths).

* Monitor students' level of involvement in sport and activity (in and out of school).

* Reduce the proportion of non-participating students in physical education.

* Provide an out-of-school-hours programme which includes a broad range of purposeful and enjoyable physical activities (competitive and non-competitive, team and individual, recreational).

* Increase the proportion of students who regularly participate in out-of-school-hours physical activities.

* Increase the proportion of staff who regularly contribute to the out-of-school-hours physical activity programme.

* Organize events (both within and beyond the curriculum) which promote physical activity (e.g. sports days, activity weeks, taster sessions).
* Identify quantitative and qualitative targets in physical education development plans that include health-related and fitness issues.

Environment (hidden curriculum)
* Provide safe, adequate and stimulating play and recreational areas (indoor and outdoor).
* Ensure that sports/activity facilities are adequate and well maintained.
* Make sports facilities and equipment available for recreational use at lunch times/break times.
* Create eye-catching physical education, sport/physical activity displays and notice boards around the physical education department and school.

Community
* Raise awareness and enlist the support of staff, parents, governors and the community to the physical activity messages being promoted within school.
* Provide all students with up-to-date, accurate information about the activity opportunities available in the local community.
* Develop alliances and partnerships with local providers (e.g. sports clubs, leisure centres) to increase the activity opportunities available.
* Provide opportunities for students, staff, governors and parents to be active.
* Formulate an Active School policy-making Committee (with student, staff, governor and parent representatives) to develop, implement and evaluate the effectiveness of the Active School Policy.

Final recommendations

In recent years, several recommendations to direct and guide physical activity promotion within schools have been published in the United Kingdom, for example by the Health Education Authority (HEA) (1998), Harris (2000), the National Audit Office (2001) and the National Heart Forum (2002). The National Institute for Health and Clinical Excellence is also currently developing guidance on promoting physical activity, play and sport for children in different settings, including in school. The guidance is due to be published in January 2009 and, whilst it will not cover the school curriculum, it is aimed at education, local authorities (as well as health professionals, the wider public, and private, voluntary and community sectors), and will include a focus on formal and informal school-based activities.

Existing recommendations share a number of common themes. In particular they support and identify the need for: (i) a whole-school approach to physical activity promotion; (ii) targeted physical activity interventions (i.e. strategies for specific groups of children); and (iii) further research into school-based approaches to promote physical activity.

Targeted interventions are recommended because children are not a homogenous group and the need to target 'needy' youngsters in particular is recognized. For example, within their policy framework 'Young and Active?' (see Chapter 4) the HEA called for interventions differentiated on the basis of gender, age and socio-economic status and identified girls aged 12 to 18 years, young people of low socio-economic status and older adolescents as priority groups.

If we can summarize, in analysing the various recommendations, a whole-school approach is recommended that incorporates the following.

◆ The development of school policies that promote healthy, active lifestyles.
◆ The provision of a supportive school and community environment that promotes and allows safe and enjoyable physical activity.
◆ Access to high quality, adequately resourced physical education designed to promote physical activity and delivered by appropriately qualified and supported staff.
◆ The promotion of health education or personal, social and health education that complements physical education.
◆ The development of inclusive out-of-school-hours physical activity programmes that feature a selection of competitive and non-competitive, structured and unstructured, team and individual activities that meet the needs and interests of all children.
◆ Access to community physical activity programmes that meet the needs and interests of all children.
◆ Adequate training for individuals who can play a role in promoting physical activity in children to help them provide appropriate, safe and enjoyable physical activity experiences.
◆ Parental education and involvement to support physical activity programmes and their children's physical activity.

References

British Heart Foundation (2007), *Healthy Schools Physical Activity booklets*. Available from the Physical Activity section of the Healthy Schools website: www.healthyschools.gov.uk

Harris, J. (2000), *Health-Related Exercise in the National Curriculum. Key Stages 1 to 4*. Champaign, IL: Human Kinetics.

Health Education Authority (1998), *Young and Active? Policy Framework for Young People and Health-Enhancing Physical Activity*. London: HEA.

National Audit Office (2001), *Tackling Obesity in England*. London: The Stationery Office.

National Heart Forum (2002), Young@Heart: *A Healthy Start for a New Generation*. London: National Heart Forum.

11 | Challenges and solutions

Introduction

In our work with teachers over the years as well as through our school-based research, we have come across a number of common issues and challenges to promoting physical activity among children. In this chapter we explore some of the general issues and challenges you are likely to face in your efforts to promote physical activity. We then outline a series of practical steps and procedures we recommend you follow when looking to influence the physical activity levels of your students. Finally, we consider some possible solutions to challenges and present you with a whole host of physical activity promotion strategies and ideas, as well as some tips and guidelines for their implementation.

Common issues

The following issues, some of which we have identified in earlier chapters, are relevant to the promotion of physical activity in children and have frequently been reported by schools and teachers. The list is by no means exhaustive but highlights just some of the challenges you may be facing. Consider which are true for you and your school.

◆ Participation in physical education is low and/or falling.
◆ Frequent non-participants are causing disruption to lessons and affecting levels of attainment and progress in physical education.
◆ Participation in out-of-school-hours physical activities is low and/or falling.
◆ Girls' participation is particularly low and/or falling.
◆ Participation at Key Stage 4 is particularly low and/or falling.
◆ The physical education curriculum is very traditional and/or not attractive or accessible to all students (e.g. it is games biased and competitive).

◆ Members of the physical education department are very traditional in terms of the policies they adopt (e.g. relating to kit, grouping procedures, curriculum).

◆ Members of the physical education department are very traditional in terms of the teaching styles they normally employ (e.g. directed approaches are most common).

◆ Physical education has low status within the school compared with other subjects.

◆ Achievement within physical education is not valued in the same way as it is in other subjects.

◆ Physical education has to compete with so many other subjects and out-of-school-hours learning opportunities (e.g. information technology, music, drama).

◆ The physical education facilities are limited and restrict the curricular and out-of-school-hours activities that can be offered.

◆ The physical education facilities are poorly managed and/or maintained.

◆ The physical education environment generally (e.g. changing rooms, corridors) is poorly managed and/or maintained.

◆ Physical education and sports equipment is limited and/or in poor condition.

◆ The physical education department is understaffed which limits the physical education programme, including the curricular and/or out-of-school-hours activities that can be offered.

◆ The physical education department works in isolation and receives little internal or external support.

◆ Other staff, including senior management are not supportive and do not get involved in physical education and school sport.

◆ Many/most parents are not supportive and/or do not get involved in physical activity and sporting opportunities.

◆ Many/most parents are not supportive of their children getting involved in physical activity and sporting opportunities.

◆ Students, especially girls, have many other responsibilities and/or commitments (e.g. homework, part-time work, household chores, child care) that restrict their participation.

Are there any other issues or challenges that you face that should be added to the list? These may relate to all students or to specific groups such as girls, Key Stage 4, ethnic minority or less able students. It may be useful to consult with colleagues on this.

Recommended practical steps and procedures

Given the above, and any other issues or groups you may have identified, the next question is where to start? When looking to promote physical activity and influence the physical activity levels of your students, we recommend that you:

1. Gather baseline or general information to establish where you and your students are currently at with respect to physical activity, and thereby what your school, department and students' needs are.
2. Decide where you want to be, in other words decide on a specific physical activity goal or goals.

Your efforts to make a difference to your students' physical activity should be realistic and built upon your school, department and students' needs, strengths and weaknesses.

Gathering information

Needs analysis

Gathering a good deal of baseline information should enable you to identify the needs of your school, your department, and your students. Ideally, you should have a clear picture about the following:

◆ students' physical activity and levels of participation within and beyond school (i.e. curricular, out of school hours);
◆ school and department policies;
◆ the physical education curriculum (including health and fitness);
◆ the out-of-school-hours programme;
◆ the physical education environment and facilities;
◆ student attainment/progress;
◆ student attitudes, motivation;
◆ staff attitudes;
◆ parent attitudes;
◆ teaching styles and strategies;
◆ community opportunities;
◆ physical education staff (strengths, skills, expertise);
◆ other schools (including feeder schools);
◆ national and local physical education/sports initiatives (see Chapter 13).

How much do you currently know about the these? Much of this information is likely to be to hand and readily available as part of your general record keeping or day-to-day work. For example, physical activity participation rates in school can be obtained from class registers and excuse notes, information about school and departmental policies can be found in the school or department prospectus and documentation, and information about students' attainment and progress is available from assessment records and reports.

Gathering some types of information may mean simply formalizing systems and procedures a little more. For example, you are no doubt very familiar with the physical education environment and facilities in your school – after all from Monday to Friday you spend most of your waking hours in the physical education department! – but how often do you scrutinize the environment in terms of how clean, tidy, warm, bright, welcoming, safe and attractive, or otherwise, it is to students? You could develop a checklist for this purpose to be completed by staff and/or students. For example, ask yourself, colleagues or your students the following questions and record the responses:

Are the sports facilities (gym, sports hall) and changing rooms:

clean?
comfortable (temperature)?
bright/cheerful?
tidy?
organized?
safe?

Do the changing rooms provide:

adequate changing space?
adequate space to hang clothes?
mirrors?
hot water?
hot showers?
soap?
privacy (e.g. cubicles, shower curtains)?

Does the physical education department:

provide clean and suitable kit available for loan?
have bright, attractive displays and notice boards?

update equipment, notice boards, displays regularly?
deliver indoor lessons in poor weather?

Any information gathering methods you use need to be simple, manageable and ideally should be built into existing policies and practices. For example, staff strengths, skills and expertise could be established when considering professional development opportunities or by conducting peer observations of teaching. Peer observations can also provide a good insight into the teaching styles and strategies most commonly employed within the department. Observe colleagues teaching and ask colleagues to observe you, and consider the extent to which they and you:

◆ use a range of teaching styles to sustain the interest of and motivate students;
◆ are sensitive to the needs and abilities of all students;
◆ provide opportunities (through different teaching styles and effective differentiation) for all students to achieve success and progress at their own level;
◆ praise effort as well as achievement;
◆ avoid 'put downs' and humiliating students;
◆ foster mutual respect between teacher–student and student–student;
◆ use a variety of appropriate grouping procedures (i.e. do not always rely on the same ones);
◆ create opportunities for students to work collaboratively;
◆ involve students in their own learning (e.g. via personal target setting, self-reflection and evaluation);
◆ involve students in leadership and other roles;
◆ encourage independence rather than dependence on the teacher.

Other information, for example researching community opportunities and national or local initiatives, or the attitudes of students, staff and parents to physical education and school sport, may not be so readily available and you may need to make a conscious effort to gather it. However, this will be time well spent. You could ask your students to gather the former information as homework or as a class activity within personal, social and health education or health-related exercise, while the latter could be established from questionnaires or from interviews with individuals or small groups. In Chapter 6 we provided some example physical activity questionnaires that focus on participation but these could be extended or developed to include questions on students' attitudes towards physical education, physical activity and sport, their likes and dislikes, and their reasons for participating or not participating in physical education, physical activity and sport.

Questions could include the following.

1. Record whether you agree (A), disagree (D), or neither agree or disagree (N), with the following statements. *(Choose a selection of statements from below, including a mix of positive and negative.)*

- Taking part in physical education, physical activity and sport at school is important
- Taking part in physical education, physical activity and sport at school is a waste of time
- Physical education is an important subject in this school
- It is cool for a girl to be active and sporty in this school
- It is cool for a boy to be active and sporty in this school
- We do too much physical education
- We do too little physical education
- Physical education and sport are too competitive
- Physical education in this school is too games based
- Physical education offers a good range of activities
- I like the activities offered in physical education
- There are not enough activities on offer at lunch time and after school
- I enjoy physical education
- I dislike physical education
- Physical education lessons are fun
- Physical education lessons are boring
- I look forward to physical education
- I dread physical education
- I feel confident in physical education
- I feel embarrassed in physical education
- I feel that I achieve success in physical education
- I feel a failure in physical education

2. List three to five things that you like about physical education and sport in your school.

3. List three to five things that you would like to change about physical education and sport in your school.

4. Complete one of the following sentences which best describes how you feel:

I would like to be involved in more physical activity but I am not because ...

OR

I would not like to be involved in more physical activity because ...

SWOT analysis

Next, we suggest that you consider the characteristics of your school, physical education department and its students that might promote, or compromise, physical activity. To do this, conduct a SWOT analysis to identify the strengths, weaknesses, opportunities and threats to your students' physical activity. This will help you to determine how effective your school or your department currently is or could be in influencing physical activity levels. Strengths and weaknesses are usually internally controlled and generated, whereas opportunities and threats are usually externally controlled and generated. For example, you might identify some of the following:

Strengths
◆ member of a successful School Sport Partnership (SSP);
◆ experienced and enthusiastic physical education staff;
◆ staff expertise in a number of activities;
◆ good indoor facilities;
◆ good participation rates among Year 7 students.

Weaknesses
◆ limited outdoor space;
◆ few non-specialist staff interested and involved;
◆ no staff expertise in dance or gymnastics;
◆ poor participation rates at Key Stage 4.

Opportunities
◆ improved links with other schools through the SSP;
◆ plans to build a new leisure centre with a pool nearby;
◆ better access to and support for professional development for physical education staff;
◆ increased budget.

Threats
◆ physical education time could be reduced;

- questionable support from senior management/governors;
- lack of parental interest/involvement;
- a large shopping centre which attracts students at lunch times and after school.

Establishing a goal

Based on both your needs and SWOT analysis, the next step is to decide on a specific and realistic physical activity goal or goals. In other words, what do you want to do, and what can you realistically achieve, regarding your students' physical activity? We recommend that you gather together your own ideas as well as the ideas and opinions of your colleagues and students. Produce a list of any common or recurring ideas or themes. Examples might include:

- a more varied and innovative physical education programme which meets the needs and interests of all students;
- all students regularly engaging in physical education;
- all students engaging in at least one out-of-school-hours physical activity per week;
- a safe, supportive, attractive and welcoming physical education environment for all students;
- physical education, physical activity and sport having higher status and support within and amongst the whole school.

Solutions and strategies

Having established the challenges, issues, needs and physical activity goal(s) for your school, the next stage is to consider some possible solutions and strategies that may help you to address these. On the following pages we present a range of solutions, strategies and ideas. These have been drawn from the information and recommendations presented in previous chapters, as well from the experience of schools that have tried and tested different initiatives and ideas. The examples represent a mixture of our own ideas which we have published elsewhere, plus ones which have been adapted from physical activity or physical education resources produced by the former Health Education Authority and the Youth Sport Trust. A number, along with other ideas, also feature or are signposted in the Physical Activity booklets mentioned in the previous chapter which support the National Healthy Schools Programme. We included some of these within the Active School Policy in

Chapter 10 but here we have built upon, added to and developed them further. The strategies are broadly grouped into the Active School categories of school and departmental policies and practices; the physical education programme (curricular and out-of-school-hours); school ethos and environment; and community links and partnerships.

A key task is to select those strategies that you feel will help you to achieve your physical activity goal(s). In addition, and as we advised in Chapter 10, you need to prioritize strategies, for example into those that are achievable in the short term, the medium term, and the long term, and choose those which you consider to be realistic, feasible and practical for your school, department and students.

School and departmental policies and practices

Develop a public relations policy that helps build the reputation of the school as being healthy and active.

Develop an Active School policy for the promotion of physical activity.

Develop physical education and PSHE policies which include HRE, physical activity and out-of-school-hours activities.

Monitor and review departmental policies on kit and showering to ensure they are not off-putting to students (e.g. make attractive, negotiate them with students).

Consider relaxing kit/uniform requirements for out-of-school-hours activities.

Monitor and review grouping policies to encourage wider participation and involvement (e.g. consider setting by ability and gender where appropriate).

Review the time of year particular activities are traditionally taught (e.g. try to avoid scheduling games in extreme temperatures and weather conditions).

Monitor and review departmental practices (e.g. in terms of variety of teaching and learning styles/approaches, a caring pedagogy).

Monitor and review staffing policies to use colleagues'

strengths appropriately (e.g. allocate staff to challenging or perpetual non-participant groups whose teaching style is empathetic with these students).

Investigate the possibility of timetabling physical education staff to remain with one particular group over a period of time. In this way, teachers will become more familiar with the students' abilities and personalities, and better able to differentiate and foster positive relationships.

Encourage senior management to consider the capabilities and willingness of applicants for all teaching posts to contribute to out-of-school-hours physical activities.

Encourage senior management to revise the school time-table to bring the start of the day forward and the end of the day earlier, enabling after school activities to finish earlier. This should enhance student safety and availability of light on winter nights, and reduce interference with students' other commitments (e.g. homework, family/work responsibilities, social activities).

Timetable lunch time activities to correspond with the year group participating in physical education directly before or following the lunch-time period or before the end of the school day. Students are more likely to take part if they are already changed and do not have to rush their lunch break.

Consider transport issues for out-of-school-hours activities (e.g. late buses or 'walking buses' for those students who remain at school for sports clubs).

Develop a school traffic policy that designates motorized traffic-free areas outside school at critical times to ensure the safety of pedestrians and cyclists.

Review and develop (if necessary) other school and departmental policies (e.g. equal opportunities, bullying, health and safety).

Identify quantitative and qualitative targets in physical education development plans that include health-related and fitness issues.

Regularly review and evaluate the effectiveness of all policies, practices and initiatives.

The physical education programme (curricular and extracurricular)

Allocate sufficient time to physical education and HRE.

Provide a broad, balanced, relevant and quality physical education programme which complies with statutory requirements and is accessible to and meets the needs and interests of all students (e.g. balance competitive and non-competitive activities, individual and team, sport and lifetime activities).

Provide an out-of-school-hours programme which includes a broad range of purposeful and enjoyable physical activities (e.g. competitive and non-competitive, team and individual, recreational).

Fully implement National Curriculum requirements for HRE through a well-structured, planned, delivered and evaluated programme of study.

Deliver the HRE knowledge base in a practical way.

Adopt student-centred, differentiated teaching and learning methods.

Promote, recognize and value the importance of having fun and taking part by de-emphasizing competition and encouraging recreational involvement and enjoyment as well, of course, as learning!

Try a sport education approach where students have opportunities to develop leadership and conflict negotiation skills by becoming referees, record keepers, reporters, coaches and administrators as well as players.

Promote safe cycling (via cycle safety and maintenance courses, cycling proficiency tests).

Find out what activity opportunities are provided for students in the community and introduce some of these within the physical education programme. Outside coaches could be employed to support physical education staff.

→ *continued*

Consider introducing new, different and more novel activities (e.g. self-defence, Pilates, indoor rowing, skateboarding, street dance, street hockey, handball, ultimate Frisbee).

Organize events (both within and beyond the curriculum) which focus on and promote physical activity (e.g. sports days, activity days/weeks, taster sessions, treasure hunts, walk/bike rides) (also see the list of ideas later in the chapter).

Introduce Sports Leadership Awards and national governing body (NGB) courses to enable older students to become leaders and officials. Encourage these students to assist with out-of-school-hours activities and other events.

Make the first week of each term a taster week for all out-of-school-hours activities.

Introduce a select-a-sport activity club. Allow students to select the activity/activities and increase the responsibility given to them to organize the club for themselves.

Offer 'drop-in' out-of-school-hours sessions which students can attend whenever they want/can, without feeling that they have to attend every week. Recognize and praise students' attendance, even if irregular.

Introduce an evening club where students return to school in the evening once they have completed their homework, looked after younger siblings, etc.

Introduce parent/carer and child, or staff and student after school clubs and activities. These should be non-competitive (e.g. aerobics, fitness, recreational swimming) and non-contact competitive activities (e.g. badminton, table tennis, swimming).

Introduce a participation card scheme where students collect signatures each time they participate in an activity in or out of school. Try to obtain suitable prizes from local businesses, sports/fitness clubs, leisure centres or community organizations (e.g. free sessions for the local swimming pool or a sports equipment or clothing voucher). Prizes could be given for the most cards completed, the best newcomer, or for introducing new members to the scheme.

→ *continued*

Introduce an incentive/award scheme along the same lines as the participation card scheme to encourage walking/cycling to school with friends and/or parents.

Offer recreational sessions aimed at students who are not team members. This will enable these students to gain skills and confidence in a safe environment.

School ethos

Promote positive attitudes towards physical education, physical activity and sport in school.

Raise awareness and enlist the support and involvement of the whole school community (e.g. students, staff, parents, governors and the community) in the promotion of physical activity and achieving physical activity goals.

Encourage a shared ownership and responsibility for the promotion of physical activity and achieving physical activity goals (e.g. among students, staff, parents, governors and the community).

Maintain the awareness of all (students, staff, parents and governors) throughout (e.g. via notices, daily briefings, letters, flyers or newsletters home, parents' evenings, staff and governor meetings).

Maintain the involvement of all (students, staff, parents and governors) throughout (e.g. encourage spectators, ask for volunteers to help out with transport, arranging events and fixtures, coaching (if suitably qualified)).

Liaise with the PSHE co-ordinator and other departments in order to promote physical activity across the curriculum (see 'Links to other curriculum areas' in Chapter 8).

Establish an entitlement for all to positive exercise experiences.

Adopt a caring pedagogy (e.g. respect for all, reward effort, inclusive teaching and grouping procedures).

→ continued

Practise equal opportunities.

Establish an Active School Committee with student, staff, governor and parent representatives to develop, implement and evaluate the effectiveness of an Active School Policy (see Guidelines for establishing an Active School Committee later).

Encourage the 'student voice' (e.g. a 'suggestion box' or a 'voice forum' on the school intranet) with regard to physical education policies and practices, the physical activity and sporting opportunities offered and the physical education environment. Feed the items raised by students into the Active School Committee.

Listen to, respect and incorporate students' feedback, comments and suggestions where possible, thereby empowering them to influence physical education policies and practices, the physical activity and sporting opportunities offered and the physical education environment.

Encourage older students to act as suitable role models and raise the status of physical education, physical activity and sport among younger students.

Recognize, reward and publicize physical activity and sports participation and achievements (e.g. via certificates, merit points, commendations, attendance/effort awards, school bulletins, assemblies).

Promote physical education, physical activity and sporting activities as widely as possible (e.g. on notice boards, in assemblies, daily briefings, newsletters, letters to parents).

Organize different physical activity and/or sports promotional events at regular intervals (e.g. one per term) (see the list of ideas later in the chapter).

Hold special assemblies and student led activities focusing on physical education, physical activity and sport.

→ *continued*

Along the lines of Sport England's Sporting Champions initiative (see Chapter 13), introduce a 'sporting ambassador's' scheme, inviting local sporting personalities or past and current students into school to serve as role models, speak in special assemblies, at celebration evenings, prize presentations or as guest coaches at special events. Ambassadors might include sports performers such as champions and medal winners, as well as individuals who have made a success of a career in sport such as physical education teachers, coaches, administrators or sports science graduates.

Use sport/physical activity (e.g. dance, gymnastics, athletics, games) as the theme for school exchange visits with students from other regions or countries.

Use physical education and sport to tackle a particular problem that may exist in your school. This might be students' attitudes towards physical education, physical activity and sport, or a whole-school issue such as attendance, behaviour or bullying.

Keep the local press informed of your efforts, achievements and the events being organized.

Conduct an audit to assess staff competencies and enthusiasm to get involved with and assist with out-of-school-hours activities.

Encourage senior management to secure funds for relevant continuing professional development (CPD) and encourage staff to attend.

Plan CPD opportunities to support teachers to develop different teaching styles and teaching and learning strategies that will encourage students' participation in physical education, physical activity and sport.

Plan opportunities for staff and parents to gain appropriate qualifications (e.g. YMCA Exercise to Music or NGB coaching awards) that will enable them to become involved in/contribute to out-of-school-hours activities.

Environment

Provide safe, adequate and stimulating play and recreational areas (indoor and outdoor).

Ensure that sports/activity facilities are adequate and well maintained.

Lobby for support for refurbishment of existing facilities and the need for new modern facilities (e.g. fitness suite, dance studio) to be included in the school facilities development plan.

Create high quality, eye-catching physical education, physical activity and sport displays and notice boards around the physical education department and the school, which are regularly updated, feature active young people enjoying physical activity and sport, and which contain relevant messages and information.

Provide clean, bright, comfortable and welcoming changing and showering facilities for students and staff. Consider installing mirrors, hair dryers and fitting shower curtains for privacy.

Brighten up the changing rooms even more with positive images of adults and young people enjoying a range of physical activities and sport (e.g. using posters or images designed and painted by students themselves).

Make sports facilities and equipment available for recreational use at lunch times/break times.

Train lunch time/break time supervisors to encourage/organize active play and physical activity.

Provide secure storage for cycles and lockers for cyclists and pedestrians.

Community links and partnerships

Investigate the physical activity and sporting provision in the local community to establish exactly what's going on and whether there is anything the school can get involved with.

Provide students with up-to-date, accurate information about the physical activity and sporting opportunities available in the local community, and encourage them to extend their physical activity and sports involvement outside school.

Establish which students from your school attend local clubs or community activities and try to enlist them as a contact person or 'buddy' for other students who might like to join.

Produce an information pack or physical activity and sports directory outlining the activities and clubs that exist in the local community. Involve students in researching the activities and clubs as a homework activity or as part of PSHE.

Develop alliances and partnerships with local providers and with organizations/individuals with particular expertise (e.g. sports clubs, leisure centres, health promotion, sports development, local businesses, coaches, exercise leaders).

Quality assure local clubs. For example, as a minimum, check that they are affiliated to their NGB and that they conform to child protection policies.

Make your physical education and sports facilities available for use by feeder schools, partner schools, local clubs and the wider community.

Consider exchanging services with local clubs. For example, trade access to your facilities with their expertise and specialist coaching.

Make use of community specialist facilities from time to time (e.g. dry ski slope, bowling alley, fitness suite).

Arrange residential school trips to outdoor education centres, national sports centres or universities. Use their facilities and expertise to provide a range of recreational and competitive activities.

→ *continued*

Liaise with local councils and health promotion specialists to develop safe play areas and walking/cycling routes to school.

Develop links and work closely with Specialist Sports Colleges, your School Sport Co-ordinator, feeder and partner schools, as appropriate.

Work with other secondary schools to pool the resources and expertise you have. It may be possible to organize some joint events and after school activities.

Work with feeder primary schools to offer after school clubs for primary children on the secondary school site. This will help to ensure that students can build on a positive experience of physical education from an early age.

If applicable, use your Year 11 sports leadership students to help run clubs for feeder primary schools. Get involved in the Step into Sport and Top Link programmes (see Chapter 13 for details of these).

Familiarize yourself with and take advantage of relevant national and local policies and initiatives which are concerned with the promotion of physical education, physical activity and sporting opportunities for children (see Chapter 13 for an overview of a selection of these).

Provide advice, guidance and counselling to students, staff, parents and governors who wish to become more active.

Provide physical activity and sporting opportunities for staff, parents and governors.

Ideas for physical activity and sports promotional events

As we noted earlier, physical activity and sports promotional events can be organized to raise the awareness, interest and involvement of students, staff, parents, governors and others in physical activity. Many of these events are also likely to provide an ideal opportunity to introduce individuals to activities they may not ordinarily think of doing, as well as be used to raise money for your school. Here we present some 'novel' as well as a few more obvious ideas for promotional events.

Swim the English Channel (31 miles) – Challenge your students to swim the English Channel. By swimming just half a mile a week, which is 32 lengths of a 25-metre pool (16 lengths twice a week), in 62 weeks, students will have swum the Channel.

Travel from Land's End to John O'Groates – Challenge your students to see whether they can walk, cycle or run from Land's End to John O'Groates. The distance is 700 miles as the crow flies. The shortest route is 848 miles. A student walking or running approximately 2.3 miles a day would get there in a year. A class of 30 each walking two miles a day would make the journey in two weeks. If this is too daunting, break the journey up and encourage students to walk or run from one major city to another. Have them check the distances between cities on a road map or the internet.

Climb Mount Everest – Mount Everest is 8,848 metres to the summit which is 58,056 steps from sea level. Challenge your students to climb Mount Everest. If they climb 160 steps a day they will have climbed it in a year. Encourage students to take the stairs (rather than the escalators or lifts) wherever possible.

The 'Iron' Triathlon – Triathlon includes three activities: swimming, cycling and running. The famous 'iron man' triathlon (or 'iron' triathlon as we prefer to call it because both men and women compete in the event!) is undoubtedly the most gruelling. It comprises a 2.4-mile swim, a 112-mile bike ride, followed by a marathon (26.2 miles) to finish. Challenge your students, in teams of three (or six to cover half the distance), to complete the equivalent triathlon as a team. Designate a team of swimmers, cyclists and runners to complete the competitive distance in their event.

'Dance Yourself Dizzy' – Organize a dance festival or evening using as many different types of dancing as you can think of which will appeal to your students (e.g. Rave, Street Dance, Salsa, Ballroom, Irish, Jazz, Asian, Rock'n'Roll), or

→ *continued*

choose a specific theme (e.g. Salsa evening). Invite a dance teacher or dance company into school to run a taster session. Alternatively, organize a dance event the whole community can enjoy such as a Square Dance or Line Dance.

'On Your Bike' Week or Month – Organize an 'on your bike' week or month during which time students are encouraged to cycle. Access the Sustran's website and their School Travel Initiatives resource, listed in Chapter 13, to obtain ideas and suggestions about organizing such an event.

Walk and Talk – Encourage your students to save on phone and 'texting' bills and arrange to meet their friends for a walk and talk. Contact the local tourist information office for maps which detail safe places to walk.

Taster Days or Sessions – Organize a taster day or series of taster sessions to give students the opportunity to try activities they have not done before. Activites might include orienteering, mountain biking, canoeing, water sports, self-defence/martial arts, Pilates, step aerobics, aqua aerobics, roller-blading.

Aerobathon – Hold an event that focuses on aerobic activity. Activities might include swimming, aerobics, step aerobics, boxercise, dancing, cycling, indoor rowing, circuits.

Skipathon – Hold an event that focuses purely on skipping (contact the British Heart Foundation 'Jump Rope for Heart' Department to make this into a fund-raising event (see Chapter 13 for further information and contact details)). There are lots of popular songs featuring the word 'jump' (e.g. Pointer Sisters, Criss Cross, House of Pain) which could be used to motivate students during the event.

Practical tips for implementing strategies

There is much advice and numerous tips we could give you for implementing physical activity strategies. Overleaf are those we consider to be the key and the most helpful for the successful implementation of strategies.

◆ Be realistic – start small with something that is manageable.
◆ Try new and different things – don't be afraid to be innovative and give things a go.
◆ Don't lose sight of your goal(s) (i.e. what you are trying to achieve) – choose strategies that will help you to achieve your goal(s) and establish specific aims, objectives and desired outcomes for them.
◆ Check availability of staff and resources – establish what staff and/ or support staff and resources are required and ensure they are adequate.
◆ Talk to and involve others – listen to and learn from the experiences of others and try to enlist their support/help.
◆ Consider training needs and implications – staff and support staff may need training in a new activity, way of working, or in matters of health and safety.
◆ Be flexible – have the confidence to make changes as the strategy develops or if it does not go according to plan.
◆ Monitor and review – establish a means for evaluating the impact of the strategy (in accordance with the aims and objectives) from the start (see 'Guidelines for monitoring and evaluation' later in this chapter).
◆ Consider strategy – adopt a strategic approach via formulating a Policy (see example in Chapter 10) which is steered by a Committee (see Guidelines below).

Guidelines for establishing an Active School Committee

Earlier and in Chapter 10, we recommended formulating a Physical Activity or Active School Policy and an Active School Committee. The reasons we gave for this were:

◆ to ensure that activity promotion is given the status it deserves and is placed and remains on your school agenda;
◆ to develop a clear vision (goal/objectives) and means (strategies) for increasing participation in physical activity;
◆ to effectively drive, co-ordinate and evaluate physical activity initiatives in your school.

In setting up an Active School Committee, general guidelines include establishing:

◆ Support – from senior management, other staff, parents, governors and students; establish where the Committee sits within the school structure.

◆ Group membership – establish group representation on the Committee (e.g. how many members (10 to 12 members is likely to be a good number), teacher/governor/parent/student mix); establish the duration and maximum period of membership – this should provide some continuity but also turnover and the flexibility for members to stand down after a period of time; establish a fair and democratic voting system (e.g. whole school, tutor group, application).

◆ Methods of operating – establish clear roles and responsibilities (e.g. chairperson, secretary, the contribution of other members); to whom the Committee will report and how often; where meetings will take place and how often.

◆ Aims of the Committee – establish clear aims and a definite focus for the Committee (e.g. aims might include reviewing issues and policy, formulating policy, organizing events, implementing strategies, monitoring and evaluation).

◆ Recognition and rewards – establish a means of recognizing and rewarding Committee members (e.g. a school badge, end-of-year social event, features/thank you letter in newsletters).

Guidelines for monitoring and evaluation

A practical tip we gave for implementing strategies was to establish a means for evaluating the impact of any strategy from the start. Monitoring and evaluation is crucial as it will enable you to:

◆ establish what worked well and/or not so well;
◆ learn from and build on the experience for your future efforts;
◆ report the outcomes to senior management, staff, governors, parents and students;
◆ on the basis of any success/improvement, lobby for future funding and support from senior management, governors, as well as external agencies;
◆ maintain interest, enthusiasm and momentum.

Strategies can be evaluated in various ways. As we recommended for the information gathering methods earlier, whatever methods you choose should be simple, manageable and ideally should form part of your everyday practice and record keeping.

First, you need to revisit the aims and objectives of the strategy to establish what outcomes or changes you are expecting. For example, if the aim of the strategy was to increase students' participation in physical activity, then the focus of the evaluation must be on participation levels and monitoring any changes over time (e.g. before and after the strategy). Depending on the aims of the strategy, you may need to gather information on changes in attitudes, participation/non-participation in physical education, attendance, attainment, the curriculum, teaching styles and methods, the teaching environment, or physical activity ethos and status. This again emphasizes the importance of the baseline information you gathered earlier to identify your school, department and students' needs.

The evaluation methods you select will clearly depend on your desired outcomes. To give you some ideas though, any of the following are possible:

◆ Registers/excuse notes – for measuring changes in attendance, participation/non-participation, attitudes.
  Excuses given for students' non-participation may reveal a lot about their motivation and attitudes towards physical education, physical activity and sport. Equally, registers could be used to record your observations concerning the motivation, attitudes or behaviour of students and classes on a daily/weekly basis.
◆ Questionnaires – for measuring changes in attitudes, physical activity levels, participation, the environment, perceived status of physical activity.
  We provided some example physical activity questionnaires in Chapter 6, as well as some example questions to measure attitude and the environment earlier in this chapter.
◆ Interviews – for measuring changes in attitudes, physical activity levels, participation/non-participation, perceived status of physical activity.
  Interviews can be formal or informal, individual or group, and can cover a wide range of issues. Whatever the format, we recommend you make and retain a record of the questions asked and the responses.
◆ Assessments of student performance/attainment – for measuring

changes in attainment, one or more of the key concepts or processes in physical education, personal learning and thinking skills (e.g. independent enquiry, team work, self-management, effective participation), confidence and self-esteem.

If interested in this method of evaluation, we suggest you employ and/or modify your school/department's existing assessment, recording and reporting procedures to illicit the information required.

◆ Teacher observations – for measuring any of the above.

You should not underestimate the value of your own or your colleagues' observations concerning students' attitudes, involvement and attainment in lessons, teaching styles and methods, as well as the environment. Your observations could be recorded periodically in your register or in a journal.

◆ Diary of events – for measuring changes in attitudes, interest, participation and involvement, the ethos or status of physical education, physical activity and sport in school.

You could keep a record of all fixtures, out-of-school-hours activities and events organized, including details of attendance, interest and involvement.

◆ Portfolio – for measuring changes in the ethos or status of physical education, physical activity and sport in school.

A portfolio could be compiled containing for example, newsletters, newspaper reports, photographs of events, letters to parents.

Whatever evaluation method(s) you employ, a final and important consideration is the timescale for collecting your information and monitoring changes. Changes are unlikely to happen overnight and it is important that you give any strategy sufficient time to take effect. For this reason, we recommend periodic follow-up evaluations, immediately after the strategy and then at regular intervals (e.g. 6 to 8 weeks) to monitor changes in the long term, as well as the sustainability or life of your efforts.

12 | Real-life examples

Introduction

Following on from the previous chapter, here we offer you some further ideas for promoting physical activity in your school. These represent real-life case study examples of projects and strategies that have been tried and tested in other schools. We have drawn the case studies from the QCA Physical Education and School Sport Investigation website (www.qca.org.uk/pess) (see Chapter 13 for further details of this programme), plus from the Healthy Schools Physical Activity Booklets (available from the Physical Activity section of the Healthy Schools website (www.healthyschools.gov.uk). The examples represent just a small selection of the numerous projects and work that schools have been involved in and aim to cover a range of different ideas and initiatives. Included are projects that have been conducted in primary and secondary schools, though the ideas are considered relevant to both contexts, and projects that have targeted the whole school, as well as some that have targeted specific groups of students (e.g. girls, Key Stage 4 students). As we recommended in Chapter 11, many of the schools have monitored the impact of their projects and have done so in various ways. For example, some of the methods used include student and teacher questionnaires, student diaries, student log books, student and teacher interviews, physical education and club registers, teacher observations, assessment and exam results and student behaviour incidents. Details of the evaluation methods and information collected by the schools involved in the QCA Physical Education and School Sport Investigation are available on the QCA website.

Case Studies

Getting pupils involved in out-of-school-hours sport

Hailsham Community College, East Sussex
The key objective of this project was to get more pupils involved in out-of-school-hours sport in order to encourage them to lead a healthier lifestyle. The school extended the range of clubs on offer before school, at lunch times and after school and coaches were employed for some activities such as judo, gymnastics, basketball and trampolining. An overtly inclusive policy was introduced for many of the clubs and they were open to all abilities and advertised as having a recreational focus. In addition, the school arranged for primary school children to work alongside Year 7 pupils in after-school clubs.

A new pastoral system was introduced that grouped pupils into houses named after famous Olympic sports stars and house matches took place every other week. It was felt that the house system gave pupils a greater sense of identity, not just with their peers, but also with pupils from other year groups.

Over a two-year period, the number of clubs the school offered increased from about 15 a week to 30 a week, and there was a large increase in the number of pupils regularly involved in out-of-hours activities, with clubs attracting high numbers each week. Teacher assessments also showed that pupils who were regularly involved in clubs developed skills more quickly than those who were not. Furthermore, an average of 60 pupils from each year group began to take part in inter-house events and pupils were reported to have developed confidence and self-esteem through their involvement in house matches.

Developing structured activities at lunchtime

Hailsham Community College, East Sussex
The objective of this project was to increase the number of pupils actively involved in structured activity during lunch times. In so doing, the school also hoped to continue to see improvements in pupils' behaviour and their ability to learn in the afternoon.

In previous years the school had found that providing structured activities for pupils led to significant improvements in their behaviour both during lunch times and in afternoon lessons and recognized that pupils were more ready to learn, more able to concentrate and more positive about learning if they had been engaged in purposeful activity. However, the school were also aware there were issues within the school building during lunch times that had to be dealt with. As a result, it was decided to offer a wider range of physical and non-physical activities during lunch times and to introduce the rule of not allowing pupils indoors during this time unless they were involved in a specific activity supervised or run by a teacher. The physical education department supervised the Astroturf area and provided indoor clubs for table tennis and dance, two other members of staff supervised an area of the school with basketball courts, and a booster trampoline class was provided for GCSE pupils.

As a consequence of the project it was reported that little negative behaviour persisted at lunch times, and afternoon lessons became more purposeful, with fewer incidents of disruption or poor behaviour. Lunch-time activity levels rose, with more than half of all pupils across year groups taking part in school sport and approximately a third being involved in physical education-related activities such as football, netball and tennis (during summer) on the Astroturf, games in the basketball area, and dance and table tennis indoors.

Establishing a healthy schools programme

Abbey Park Middle School, Worcestershire

Through this project, the school's objective was to increase the number of pupils making healthy lifestyle choices, including about exercise. The school also hoped to improve pupils' behaviour at lunch times. The school employed a supervisor who was given responsibility for promoting and developing physical activity at break times and lunch times through a 'Huff and Puff' programme. The supervisor was trained and supported in how to organize and develop purposeful play, including communication and organizational skills, different ideas for activities and how to organize and use space. The supervisor's main tasks were to organize the activities in the playground and to oversee Year 7 pupils who ran the equipment loan shop. Pupils bought a key-ring which they could then use as a deposit for equipment borrowed from the shop.

The supervisor's work was supported by circle time developed through the behaviour support services, including a 'life skills' project, and by the school nurse who was invited to run drop-in sessions. The nurse was kept fully informed about out-of-school-hours sport activities and counselled and encouraged the children to join in. This ensured the supervisor had the support she needed, that messages were reinforced effectively, and that break times and lunch times were seen as part of the learning that took place each day. The school also introduced a reward system for pupils who reached set activity targets by giving them play equipment bought through sponsorship from local businesses.

The school found that pupils who did not take part in out-of-school-hours sport in the past, including several who were overweight, joined in with the 'Huff and Puff' scheme. Also, once the supervisor started work, the number of serious incidents of negative behaviour in the playground halved, saving considerable time for senior staff. Pupils were reported to be noticeably more co-operative and tolerant of each other, and there was less disruption in lessons and during the changeover between lessons.

Getting girls involved in physical education and school sport

Wright Robinson Sports College, Manchester

The objective of this project was to increase girls' participation in extracurricular sports clubs and give them the opportunity to experience sports they would not normally take part in at school. The girls were given a questionnaire which asked them to select the sports and activities they would most like to participate in during lessons and extracurricular time during a special 'girls' week'. The most popular three or four activities selected by the girls in each physical education group and the most popular extracurricular activities were noted and a curriculum timetable was devised for the week. Experts from outside the college were invited to deliver sessions on street dance, self-defence and football, while other sessions were planned and delivered by physical education staff. An extensive extracurricular timetable was also designed which included off-site activities such as golf and rock-climbing and again involved experts from the community delivering a number of the activities (e.g. football, self-defence, break and street dance, golf, gymnastics, netball, cheerleading, rock-climbing).

Pupils were able to select up to three different activities to try during their physical education sessions that week. As an incentive to encourage girls to take part in the extracurricular activities on offer, a passport scheme was introduced with prizes ranging from beauty products to sports equipment. Girls were given a passport when they first attended a club and received a stamp for every club they attended during the week. When they had gained three stamps they were entitled to a small prize (e.g. pens, make-up samples, hair bands), six stamps earned them a bigger prize (e.g. socks, balls, boot bags, water bottles), and ten stamps entitled them entry to the prize draw for a larger prize. During the week pupils were also allowed to wear their own sports clothes rather than physical education kit. After discussion with the girls some changes were also made to their changing facility to introduce liquid soap, soft toilet tissue, hairdryers, a better-fitting shower curtain and six new mirrors. The changing rooms were also decorated with balloons, streamers and ribbons to make the week noticeably different.

The girls were reported to have responded positively to the week, the verbal feedback received was excellent, and there was a great increase in extracurricular participation, particularly at lunch times, with more than 70 girls attending. The most popular sessions were those that were new to the pupils (e.g. rock-climbing, break dance, boxercise) and those that were relaxed and non-competitive (e.g. tennis, swimming, a friendly rounders tournament). The changes made to the changing rooms were also greatly appreciated and the hairdryers and correctly fitting shower curtain led to even more girls than usual wanting to swim.

Regrouping pupils and redeploying staff

Wright Robinson Sports College, Manchester

The primary objective of this project was to raise attainment in physical education by improving pupils' progress. The school also hoped to see an improvement in behaviour in physical education lessons. The school decided to group Key Stage 3 pupils by ability after they had completed their transition work. If appropriate, the school then changed these groups at the start of Key Stage 4, based on end of Key Stage 3 records of progress, achievement and attainment. GCSE pupils were grouped for GCSE theory based on National Curriculum test scores and on evidence from science and English cognitive ability tests.

The school also looked very carefully at the allocation of staff to teaching groups. All teachers in the physical education department were observed and it was discovered that some were best at getting the most out of less able groups, while others worked best with the more able. The school worked with Manchester's Education Partnership, including the physical education adviser and the head of department, to obtain an external review of all teaching and learning. As a result of this, the school took into consideration the strengths of individual teachers when deciding who should teach which groups.

In addition, the school identified target setting as a major area of development. All pupils were provided with clear attainment targets and at Key Stage 4 this was enhanced by a comprehensive mentoring programme. In particular, the school focused on borderline A* and C/D pupils, as well as working extensively with supposed 'at risk' individuals.

Within one year, attainment in physical education was found to have improved across both Key Stages. At the end of Key Stage 3, pupils continued to perform above the national average, with improvements year on year. At Key Stage 4, GCSE physical education and dance results improved and the college A*–C rose from 29 per cent to 43 per cent.

The school felt that grouping pupils according to their ability helped them all to feel included and successful. Teachers were better able to plan lessons to match pupils' needs and to allow every pupil to make progress. Consequently, pupils' self-esteem and motivation increased and they enjoyed physical education more. Also, having made changes to pupils' groupings and their teachers, no serious behaviour incidents in physical education lessons were encountered.

Motivating pupils with tailor-made pathways

Peacehaven Community School, East Sussex

The objective of this project was to maintain pupils' interest in and positive attitudes towards physical education throughout Key Stage 4. The school wanted to ensure that pupils' high levels of participation and motivation in Key Stage 3 physical education continued into Key Stage 4. It was decided to try to achieve this by offering a wide range of activities at Key Stage 4 with different pathways through the activities. Towards the end of the year, a questionnaire was administered to all Year 9 pupils which listed the physical education activities on offer and asked them to identify which they would like to do. The pupils were also asked whether they would prefer a course that focused on competing and performing (a team performance route), developing personal fitness (an individual performance route), or promoting health and well-being through recreation (a social route). Pupils were also given the option to be assessed in different ways such as through performing, coaching, umpiring or leading. In addition, some were able to take a Sports Leader Award. Upon completion of the questionnaires, one-to-one sessions were held with pupils to give them guidance on which pathway would best suit their strengths. This approach helped most pupils to select courses they were going to succeed at and enjoy.

With the range of activities and new pathways offered, pupils' enthusiasm for physical education was found to be excellent and 82 per cent reported that they enjoyed the subject more than in Key Stage 3. Furthermore, participation was 100 per cent, pupils arrived to lessons on time and ready to work, and commitment to the courses they had chosen was high. Furthermore, it was felt that the small number of lesson disruptions that had been experienced previously were eliminated because pupils had been able to choose courses and pathways that suited them and which they wanted to undertake.

Pupils take charge of inter-house sport

Earls High School, Halesowen, Dudley

The objectives of this project were to increase pupils' participation in out of school hours sport and to improve their leadership and citizenship skills by giving them opportunities to run activities. Although the overall participation rate in out-of-school-hours sport at the school was not particularly low, provision was limited to football, rugby, cricket and rounders and the inter-house system was in serious decline. Furthermore, house leaders, appointed on a voluntary basis, had little time available to promote sport and pupils were becoming increasingly disenchanted with school sport, viewing it as largely the preserve of the gifted and talented. Around 75 per cent of pupils reported in an end of Key Stage questionnaire that they wanted better and wider extracurricular provision for all.

In response, the school set itself the target of increasing participation in out-of-hours sport by at least 10 per cent. Following a curriculum review, it also looked at using out of hours activities as a vehicle for developing pupils' citizenship and leadership skills. To achieve this, overall responsibility for inter-house activities was given to the school's sports council, which was made up of captains from years 10 and 11 and physical education prefects from years 7 to 9. The council met once a week to organize and oversee sports competitions, refereeing, coaching and the promotion of sport across the school. To support these changes, two leadership courses were introduced, the Sports Leaders Award and the Step into Sport scheme. The range of out-of-school-hours activities available was also increased and netball, hockey, ultimate Frisbee, table tennis, basketball, inter-house gymnastics, dance, cheerleading, inter-house athletics and trampolining were added to the four established sports, with specialist staff coming in to oversee the individual sports and provide help where needed. As part of their marketing of inter-house activities, the sports council revamped the inter-house sports notice board and a confidential 'good news board' was set up in the staff room to keep all staff informed of pupils' involvement in out-of-school-hours activities, the sports council and leadership initiatives.

The school exceeded its target for participation in out-of-hours sport. Both the Sports Leaders Award and the Step into Sport scheme was a success and a number of Key Stage 4 pupils improved their evaluation and attainment by a level, which was considered attributable to their increased participation in out-of-hours sport. Furthermore, the pupils involved in the sports council developed excellent citizenship and leadership skills, negotiating all aspects of inter-house sports events in weekly meetings. Pupils across the school approached the sports council for information and advice on how to become involved and the majority of pupils were keen to consult the inter-house sport notice boards. The council members took every opportunity to promote events and to persuade formerly reluctant participants to join in, and increasing numbers of formerly demotivated or uninterested pupils began regularly participating in inter-house events.

Grangefield Comprehensive School

A meeting of the Healthy School Task Group identified a need to address the school travel theme of the National Healthy Schools Programme, as traffic congestion was busy on the main road to the school and there was no cycle storage available for pupils. The Stockton Borough Council School Travel Plan Champion was invited to a Healthy School Task Group meeting to advise on a way forward. Working in partnership with the school, a travel survey and basic audit was carried out with the children and parents/carers and the results were used to formulate an action plan for developing a School Travel Plan.

A bid for funding was sought (with the assistance of Sustrans) from the cycling projects fund, to provide drying and showering facilities for cyclists travelling in wet weather. Funding for the development of cycle routes was obtained from the local transport plan sources and Safer Routes to School funding supported the purchase of bicycle lockers. Links were made to promote safer cycling and walking with new Year 6 pupils, and further funding was accessed to print an independent travel brochure for the children and their parents/carers from the feeder primaries to help with transition between schools.

Florence Melly Community Primary School

Children, staff, parents/carers and governors at the school worked together to make the school journey and the school environment safer. The travel team worked with Travelwise and the local police to examine travel problems relating to the school and drew up a plan of traffic-calming measures within the vicinity. As part of whole-school involvement, the curriculum was also adapted so that areas such as geography (under studies of the local area) included a detailed study of the travel situation, allowing for cross-curricular links to be made between geography and personal, social and health education. As a result, a group of Year 5 and 6 children worked on a 'Walk to School' project which included the making of a video demonstrating some of the dangers when walking to school. This was accompanied by a map which was produced to show the area around the school, annotated with areas that needed to be made safer with road traffic-calming measures.

References

British Heart Foundation (2007), *Healthy Schools Physical Activity Booklets*. Booklets A and B. Available from the Physical Activity section of the Healthy Schools website: www.healthyschools.gov.uk

Qualifications and Curriculum Authority (QCA), *Physical Education and School Sport Investigation Website* (www.qca.org.uk/pess)

V | How? – Beyond the School

13 | Opportunities and support

Introduction

Government, commercial organizations and charitable trusts have developed a number of initiatives and resources to support the promotion and development of physical activity and sporting opportunities for children in recent years. In this chapter, we look at some of the more formal opportunities and support available to assist you in your work and we provide details of a number of government and non-government national school-based or school-centred physical activity and/or sporting initiatives, and relevant resources, websites and contacts. The examples are far from exhaustive but we aim to cover some of the key, as well as reflect the range of support available.

It is worth pointing out at this stage however, that, perhaps more so than at any other time, government and other initiatives are constantly changing and developing. This makes it a very exciting time for everyone involved in working with children, as well, of course, for the youngsters themselves. We advise you therefore to try to keep abreast of developments, for example through membership of your subject association, the Association for Physical Education (AfPE), and by taking advantage of relevant professional development opportunities, reading professional journals such as *Physical Education Matters*, and routinely accessing relevant websites. Indeed, the information we present here has been accessed from the relevant organizations' websites, a list of which we have compiled in Table 13.3.

Government strategies and associated initiatives

The Physical Education and Sport Strategy for Young People (formerly the Physical Education, School Sport and Club Links Strategy)

The government has shown an unprecedented commitment to physical education and sport in schools via the Physical Education and Sport Strategy for Young People (PESSYP) (which was formerly launched and known as the Physical Education, School Sport and Club Links Strategy (PESSCL)). The PESSCL Strategy was launched in October 2002 to 'transform physical education and school sport' and was initially supported by government investment of £459 million over three years, which was then extended to £978 million until 2008. The Department for Children, Schools and Families and the Department for Culture, Media and Sport are jointly leading the strategy, the overall objective of which is to enhance the take up of sporting opportunities by 5 to 16 year olds. The initial target, which, as noted in Chapter 4 has been met, was:

> to ensure that 75 per cent of children do two hours of high quality physical education and school sport a week by 2006 and 85 per cent by 2008.

Currently, the government's ambition for 2010 is:

> to ensure that all children should have two hours of curriculum physical education and the opportunity to access a further two to three hours of sport beyond the curriculum per week.

This is being referred to as the 'five hours a week' target.

> The Strategy is being delivered through nine interlinked pro-grammes which include:
> Specialist Sports Colleges
> School Sport Partnerships
> Professional Development
> Step into Sport
> Club Links
> Gifted and Talented
> Sporting Playgrounds
> Swimming

Qualifications and Curriculum Authority's (QCA) Physical Education and School Sport Investigation.

The first two, Sports Colleges and School Sport Partnerships, have created a national physical education and school sports infrastructure by establishing a network of School Sport Partnerships (families of schools which work together to enhance physical education and sports opportunities for all). The remaining seven programmes are the tools the schools and partnerships draw on to enable children to take up the sporting opportunities and achieve the government's targets.

Specialist Sports Colleges

Specialist Sports Colleges were first introduced in 1997 as part of the Specialist Schools Programme run by the Department for Education and Skills (now the Department for Children, Schools and Families). The programme helps schools to establish distinctive identities through their chosen specialism (i.e. sport) and achieve targets to raise standards. Any maintained secondary school in England can apply to become a Specialist School and will be awarded specialist status if they meet the standard to enter the programme. In return, the school receives additional capital and funding. Sport is one of ten specialisms within the Specialist Schools Programme. The vision for Specialist Sports Colleges is to raise standards of achievement in physical education and sport for all students leading to whole school improvement. They are expected to develop a visible sports ethos throughout the school and within their local community and to provide a regional focal point for promoting excellence in physical education and community sport. For example by extending links between families of schools, sports bodies and communities, sharing resources, developing and spreading good practice and helping to provide a structure through which young people can progress to careers in sport and physical education.

School Sport Partnerships

As already noted, School Sport Partnerships are families of schools that work together to enhance physical education and sports opportunities for all. The overall aim of School Sport Partnerships is to help schools to enable their pupils to spend a minimum of two hours each week on high quality physical education and school sport.

Each partnership is individual but in developing new partnerships and expanding existing partnerships, a typical partnership model is promoted. Partnerships are usually made up of a Specialist Sports College, up to eight secondary schools, and around 45 primary or special schools, clustered around the secondary schools and Specialist Sports College. Each partnership receives a substantial grant each year to support specific posts and teacher release. The posts include a full-time Professional Development Manager, usually based in a Sports College, whose role is to strategically develop and manage the partnership, and School Sport Co-ordinators, based in secondary schools, who concentrate on improving school sport opportunities, including out-of-hours learning, across the family of schools. In addition, Primary Link Teachers based in primary and special schools aim to improve the quantity and quality of physical education and sport in their own schools.

Competition Managers are also funded to work across the network of School Sport Partnerships. Their role is to plan, manage and implement a programme of inter-school competition across their partnership and against others. They also reach out into national governing body school sports competitions.

Professional Development

Given the focus of the PESSYP Strategy on 'high quality physical education and school sport', the professional development of teachers and others would seem to be paramount to ensuring this is achieved. The Physical Education and School Sport Professional Development programme seeks to ensure that physical education teachers have the tools and expertise needed to inspire and engage children and young people.

The programme aims to:

◆ improve the quality of teaching and learning in physical education and school sport in order to raise pupils' attainment and increase the amount of sport youngsters do;

◆ increase the understanding of how high quality physical education and school sport can be used as a tool for whole-school improvement;

◆ improve the understanding of how high quality physical education and school sport can be used to support healthy lifestyles and physical activity;

◆ encourage more innovative interpretation of the physical education programme of study to better meet the needs of all pupils to enhance achievement;

◆ enhance cross-phase continuity to improve pupils' progress.

The programme focuses on the creation of nationally developed modules and resources which are delivered locally through local delivery agents and/or School Sport Partnerships.

Step into Sport

Step into Sport seeks to increase the number of young people aged 14 to 19 from School Sport Partnerships actively involved in sports leadership and volunteering. It provides a clear framework of co-ordinated opportunities at a local level to enable young people to begin and sustain an involvement in leadership and volunteering through sport. In schools, pupils can experience sports leadership, gain leadership qualifications, help children in primary schools organize festivals of sport, and take up sports volunteering placements in their communities. At the same time, national governing bodies in a range of sports are being supported to develop and implement volunteering strategies to ensure the effective deployment, development and recognition of their volunteers in community sports clubs.

Club Links

The main aim of the Club Links Programme is to strengthen links between schools and local sports clubs and by doing so increase the number of children who are members of, or participate in, governing body or other accredited sports clubs. The programme is being delivered through the governing bodies of 22 sports, including athletics, badminton, basketball, canoeing, cricket, cycling, football, golf, gymnastics, hockey, judo, netball, orienteering, rowing, rugby league, rugby union, sailing, squash, swimming, table tennis, tennis and volleyball.

In addition, multi-skill clubs have been set up for primary school children to provide them with additional opportunities to develop fundamental physical skills and to act as a stepping-stone into club sport. Dance links are also being developed with the National Dance Teachers Association and Youth Dance England.

Gifted and Talented

The principle aim of the Gifted and Talented Programme is to improve the identification of gifted and talented pupils and to enhance support and provision for such pupils in physical education and school sport. Action is divided into four key areas.

1. Benchmarking Excellence – Gifted and Talented Physical Education Quality Standards are being developed which are complemented by online support materials for schools and local authorities to help them achieve the standards. There will also be professional development for teachers to help them support talented young people within physical education.
2. Talent Identification in Physical Education – Research was undertaken by Leeds Metropolitan University and Christ Church Canterbury to identify the components of talent and this is being used to inform all the other programmes and help teachers identify talented young people in their schools.
3. Provision for talented young athletes – A network of Multi-skill Academies has been established for young people in School Sport Partnerships designed to help young people with identified talent to develop the core skills that are the basis of all sports. Also a number of National Governing Bodies of Sport have been supported to deliver performance camps for their elite young athletes.
4. Support for talented athletes – Talent support programmes are now operating in many School Sport Partnerships to help them effectively support talented young people. This involves the Junior Athlete Education (JAE) programme, which trains and supports young people and teachers in lifestyle management and performance planning. The programme involves the identification of trained adult JAE mentors who support the talented young athletes in their relationships with their coach, teachers and parent/carers. In addition, an on-line Profiling and Tracking system is available to enable schools to enhance the support they offer.

Sporting Playgrounds

Since 2001, the government has been working with the Youth Sport Trust to support three phases of playground development in primary schools across England. Playground projects have been developed and piloted based on a Zoneparc model in an effort to increase physical activity levels and improve behaviour.

The Zoneparc model zones the playground into three coloured areas for different types of activity so that certain activities cannot dominate the space. The red zone is for more traditional, active sport, the blue provides a multi-activity area and the yellow is a quiet play area. In this way, it is hoped to make the playground accessible to many more pupils and to those who may otherwise have been intimidated during play times. Zoneparc also introduces innovative play equipment and resources, and young play leaders and lunch time supervisors are trained to distribute equipment and organize games and activities.

Swimming

Swimming and water safety are statutory activities at Key Stage 2, designed to ensure children are able to swim unaided over a distance of at least 25 metres. The swimming strand within the Strategy aims to try to ensure more children reach this target by the end of Key Stage 2. Actions include the following:

> The publication of a *Swimming Charter* which provides practical advice on how to plan and deliver effective swimming programmes. It also provides guidance on how to encourage more children to take up and enjoy swimming.

> The creation of a Swimming and Water Safety website. The site, which was developed by the QCA, is aimed at teachers, parents and pupils and provides practical ideas, resources and guidance to help children and young people learn how to swim safely and well.

> Running pilot Swimming Top-Up Schemes to try to establish how children who were likely to reach the end of their primary schooling without being able to swim could be supported to learn and enjoy the sport.

As a result of the success of the pilots further investment in the programme has been made to fund a national Top-Up swimming programme. To support the organizer of the scheme a Top-Up Swimming Toolkit has also been developed and schools will receive support from the Amateur Swimming Association.

QCA's Physical Education and School Sport Investigation

Another key programme is QCA's Physical Education and School Sport (PESS) Investigation which we briefly mentioned in Chapter 12. Since 2000, the QCA has been working with primary, secondary, special schools and partnerships across England to develop ways of improving the quality of PESS and explore the difference that high quality PESS can make to young people and their schools.

The schools and partnerships involved in the investigation are aiming to ensure that all of their pupils spend a minimum of two hours each week on high-quality physical education and school sport. At the same time, each school and partnership has selected one or more whole-school improvement objectives that it would like to achieve through investing in PESS (ranging from improved progress and attainment in PESS, to improved behaviour and attendance). These broader objectives influence the strategies that the schools and partnerships are using, which include:

◆ redesigning the physical education curriculum;
◆ developing break and lunch times to provide purposeful skill and health-enhancing activities;
◆ making the most of time for physical education and school sport related activities before and after school;
◆ supporting and developing teachers, other adults and young leaders;
◆ investing in equipment and facilities for PESS.

All of the schools and partnerships involved in the PESS investigation have been reported to have benefited from the project. All achieved the initial target of 75 per cent of their pupils taking part in a minimum of two hours of high quality PESS each week. Furthermore specific improvements have been seen in the following areas: progress and attainment in physical education and school sport; increased involvement in healthy, active lifestyles; behaviour; attendance; attitudes to learning; attainment across the curriculum; leadership skills; citizenship qualities; and inclusion in physical education and school sport.

In Chapter 12 we provided details of some of the projects and initiatives schools have been involved in through the PESS Investigation, including the outcomes. For information about other projects, access the case studies on the QCA's website: www.qca.org.uk/pess.

Sport England and associated initiatives

Sport England has and continues to be instrumental in supporting the development of sports and physical activity opportunities for children and has developed a number of initiatives over the years. An example of a current Sport England initiative is Sporting Champions.

Sporting Champions

Sporting Champions is a unique scheme that aims to inspire young people to be more active and take part in sport on a regular basis by giving them the chance to meet their sporting heroes. Around 450 visits each year are organized which bring world-class athletes from a wide range of sports into schools and local communities throughout the country. The main goal is to show young people that sport can and should be fun and to sow the seeds that will start a lifelong enjoyment of physical activity.

In terms of benefits, it is proposed that a Sporting Champions visit will:

◆ raise awareness of sport and the benefits of physical activity;
◆ engage and enthuse young people;
◆ increase the profile of a variety of sports and local sports clubs;
◆ improve behaviour in the local community;
◆ motivate young people in their wider lives;
◆ raise the profile of a particular event.

The visits can be tailored to fit the needs of the school or community group and can involve interactive question and answer sessions, sporting demonstrations, coaching workshops or targeted activity such as contributing to the leadership and volunteering agenda.

The National Healthy Schools Programme

The National Healthy Schools Programme (NHSP) is a joint Department of Health and Department for Children, Schools and Families initiative. As we highlighted in Chapter 10, the vision of the programme is for all children and young people to be healthy and achieve at school and in life. The specific aims of the NHSP are:

◆ to support children and young people in developing healthy behaviours;
◆ to help raise achievement;
◆ to help reduce health inequalities;
◆ to help promote social inclusion.

Further details of the programme can be found in Chapter 10.

Non-government initiatives

Safe Routes to School

Safe Routes to School is an initiative developed by Sustrans, the sustainable transport charity. Safe Routes to School projects encourage and enable children to walk and cycle to school through a combined package of practical and educational measures. The initiative also strives to improve road safety and reduce child casualties, improve children's health and development, and reduce traffic congestion and pollution.

Safe Routes to School projects are about working together as a community to make the school journey safer and healthier and involve the whole-school community, local residents, local authorities, health and education workers and the police. Example projects include providing school safety zones with 20mph speed limits, 'walking buses', safe cycle storage or lockers for cyclists/pedestrians, cycle or pedestrian training, or organizing 'walk to school' or 'road safety' weeks. Sustrans runs a national Safe Routes to School information service and provide training, videos, newsletters, factsheets, teachers packs, resources, advice and networking opportunities. The Safe Routes to School Project also has its own website which provides information about School Travel Plans and Safe Routes to School projects.

Bike It

Bike It is another Sustrans project which is working to increase the number of children who cycle to school. The project has a manager, regional supervisors and a number of officers who work with schools to facilitate safe and independent cycling to school. Teachers have reported Bike It to have transformed their schools and children to be energized, excited, ready to learn and travelling safely and independently. Many parents also join in the bike events and school projects, helping to run bike clubs, accessing the information on safe cycling, and helping their children to receive cycle training in school.

Jump Rope for Heart

Jump Rope for Heart is a British Heart Foundation sponsored skipping challenge. It aims to promote healthy exercise among children, raise funds for the BHF and the schools or groups taking part, and encourage teachers to develop physical activity opportunities. Schools or groups who register for the initiative receive a free Jump Rope for Heart skipping kit which contains skipping ropes, a skipping skills DVD, a teacher's manual and other materials. An optional workshop is also offered to teachers.

TOP programmes

The TOP programmes have been developed by the Youth Sport Trust and are a series of linked and progressive schemes for all young people aged 18 months to 18 years. The programmes form a sporting pathway along which children can progress according to their age and development, providing the tools required for the delivery of high quality physical education and school sport. Resource cards, child-friendly equipment and training and support for teachers and deliverers are key features of the TOP programmes. Programmes include TOP Tots, TOP Start, TOP Play, and Sainsbury's TOP Activity Programmes (for pre-school through to primary), TOP Link (for secondary), and TOP Sportsability.

TOP Link

TOP Link encourages 14- to 16-year-old students to organize and manage sport or dance festivals in local primary and special schools and is designed to enhance and improve links between schools. TOP Link is also part of the PESSYP Step into Sport programme (see earlier) and is linked to existing leadership work in schools such as the Level 1 and Level 2 Sports Leaders Awards. All participating schools are able to send their students to a one-day leadership conference in their region. The young people work in teams to plan and organize a festival of sport or dance before staging it for their local primary or special school, usually in the summer term.

TOP Sportsability

TOP Sportsability is targeted specifically at young people with disabilities and provides opportunities for the integration of disabled and non-disabled young people in unique sports challenges. Inclusion of all is a priority and the programme creates opportunities for children with disabilities to enjoy, participate and perform in physical education and sport. This is achieved through a series of inclusive equipment sets and resource cards. There are five inclusive games within the programme: boccia, goalball, polybat, table cricket and table hockey, and these are accompanied by resource cards which include both information on playing each of the games and a number of different inclusive activities. As with the other TOP programmes, TOP Sportsability offers teacher training on the effective use of the TOP Sportsability resource cards, equipment and handbook.

Personal Best Challenge Parks

Developed with Coca-Cola and in partnership with the British Olympic Foundation, Personal Best Challenge Parks utilize school breaks and lunch times to encourage secondary age students to participate in physical activity. Focused on the Olympic value of achieving one's best, the aim of the parks is to increase interest and participation in physical activity for all children and not just those who show a natural ability in sport. School playgrounds are transformed in an attempt to make them more active, enjoyable, healthy and safe for young people to enjoy before, during and after school. The project also offers training and resources to support students and staff in school.

Sky Living For Sport

Developed in partnership with BSkyB, Living For Sport endeavours to use the power of sport to engage young people and to motivate and inspire them to reach their full potential. The project targets young people aged 11 to 16 who are at risk of opting out of school life, whether through poor attendance or lack of confidence. Participating schools select the groups of young people to be involved. Students then work with their teachers and support staff to set personal targets and goals and, after taking part in a range of diverse activities such as sailing, archery and martial arts, they go on to organize a sporting event for a local school or community group. These have been diverse and wide ranging and have included events such as inter-school tournaments and dance performances. The schools are also offered a series of visits by a sporting hero and the project culminates with a celebration event, recognizing and rewarding the young people's achievements against their set goals.

More recently, two new strands to the project focusing on schools and parents have been developed, along with a Continued Professional Development toolkit for schools not participating in the project. The toolkit comprises resources on a CD-ROM which provide teachers with the information, materials and guidance on how to implement the initiative.

Norwich Union GirlsActive

Norwich Union GirlsActive is spearheaded by Double Olympic gold medal winner, Dame Kelly Holmes. The project is designed to empower teenage girls to enjoy more sporting activity on their own terms by allowing them to make positive choices and giving them a voice. It also strives to enable young people to make a positive contribution to their schools. Girls are challenged to come up with ideas on what they would change in their own schools in order to make sporting activity something they would want to participate in.

A number of GirlsActive roadshows have taken place across the country for targeted schools, where girls aged 13 to 16 have been given the opportunity to take part in taster sessions in activities such as street dance, boxercise and rock-climbing. Girls were also challenged to work with their teachers to identify the issues surrounding girls' participation, to take the lead in addressing the issues, and to encourage their school peers to become and stay more active.

Dreams + Teams

Dreams + Teams is run in conjunction with the British Council and is active in 46 countries. The project aims to develop mutual under-standing between countries regarding the use of sport in helping to develop education and leadership skills and cross-cultural awareness in 14 to 18 year olds through sport and international educational links. The project explores issues such as fair play, equity, cultural diversity, inclusion, religion, ethics and global communication and culminates in a festival offering young people the opportunity to showcase their work together.

Schools on the Move

Schools on the Move is a Department of Health-funded programme developed by the Youth Sport Trust in partnership with the British Heart Foundation. It is a school-based pedometer promotion for 9- to 13-year-olds designed to encourage pupils to become more active. The programme uses pedometers in a fun way to raise awareness of the role of physical activity in maintaining health and well-being and provides schools with the tools to help promote and focus on physical activity.

The programme is also supported by a Schools on the Move website (www.schoolsonthemove.co.uk) which offers a variety of interactive features, ideas and support materials for pupils, teachers and health professionals working with schools.

Useful resources, websites and contacts

There are a number of resources and teacher and student websites available to support you and we provide details of just a selection of these along with a list of useful contact organizations in Tables 13.1, 13.2, and 13.3. As we noted earlier, the lists, and particularly the resources list, are by no means exhaustive but aim to present a flavour of what is available. The resources included are considered relevant either to the National Curriculum or to physical activity promotion practice, and the content is consistent with the key messages and philosophy we advocate throughout this book.

Table 13.1 Useful resources

Useful Resources
British Heart Foundation (2000), *The Active School Resource Packs for Primary and Secondary Schools*. London: British Heart Foundation. Available from: www.bhf.org.uk/publications.aspx
British Heart Foundation (2007), *Healthy Schools Physical Activity Booklets*. Available on the physical activity section of the Healthy Schools website: www.healthyschools.org.uk
Cale, L. and Harris, J. (2005), *Young people and physical activity. Issues, Implications and Initiatives*. Basingstoke: Palgrave Macmillan.
Continyou (2005), *Breakfast Movers Essential Guide*. Can be downloaded by visiting: www.continyou.org.uk/what_we_do/children_and_young_people/breakfast_club_plus/keeping_it_going/resources
Continyou (2008), *PE and Sport Out-of-School-Hours Learning Guide*. Can be downloaded by visiting: www.continyou.org.uk
DfES (2006), *School Club Links Guide*. To access visit: www.teacher-net.gov.uk/_doc/9740/schoolclublinks[1].pdf
Elbourn, J. (2004), *Fitness Room Activities in Secondary Schools*. Leeds: Coachwise 1st4Sport. Available at: www.1st4sport.com/
Elbourn, J. (2008), *Aerobics and Circuits for Secondary Schools*. Leeds: Coachwise 1st4Sport. Available at: www.1st4sport.com/
Harris, J. (2000), *Health-Related Exercise in the National Curriculum*. Leeds: Human Kinetics. Available at: www.1st4sport.com/
Harris, J. and Elbourn, J. (2002), *Warming Up and Cooling Down*. Leeds: Human Kinetics. Available at: www.1st4sport.com/
Sustrans (2006), *School Travel Initiatives: A Practical Guide to Pupil Participation*. Can be downloaded by visiting: www.sustrans.org.uk/default.asp?sID=1208345865073

Table 13.2 Relevant teacher and student websites

Website	Description
Teacher	
www.active.org.uk	A physical activity promotion website.
www.bbc.co.uk/health/	The BBC health website which provides information on various health issues.
www.healthyschools.gov.uk	The National Healthy Schools Programme website providing information about Healthy Schools, resources and support materials.
www.sheu.org.uk	The Schools Health Education Unit website which provides lifestyle surveys, research and publishing services, including information about young people's health-related behaviour.
www.teachernet.gov.uk/teaching andlearning/subjects/pe	Provides information, news and updates on the Physical Education and Sport Strategy for Young People (PESSYP).
Student	
www.need2know.co.uk/health	A website for secondary students which gives young people information about health and a range of health issues/topics.
www.playgroundfun.org.uk	An interactive website which includes games to play, ideas for play and information on building games. The site can also be used by teachers and parents.

Table 13.3 Useful contact organizations and their websites

Association for Physical Education	www.afpe.org.uk
British Heart Foundation (BHF)	www.bhf.org.uk www.bhfactive.org.uk
BHF National Centre for Physical Activity and Health	www.bhfactive.org.uk/young-people
Children's Play Council	www.ncb.org.uk/cpc
English Federation of Disability Sport	www.efds.net
Institute of Youth Sport	www.lboro.ac.uk/departments/ sses/institutes/iys
National Dance Teachers Association	www.ndta.org.uk
National Institute for Health and Clinical Excellence	www.nice.org.uk
Qualifications and Curriculum Authority	www.qca.org.uk www.qca.org.uk/pess
Sports Coach UK	www.sportscoachuk.org
Sport England	www.sportengland.org
Sports Leaders UK	www.sportsleaders.org
Sustrans	www.sustrans.org.uk
Women's Sports and Fitness Foundation	www.wsf.org.uk
Youth Dance England	www.yde.org.uk
Youth Sport Trust	www.youthsporttrust.org
YMCA Fitness Industry Training Central YMCA Qualifications (CYQ)	www.ymcafit.org.uk www.cyq.org.uk

Points to note

Evidently then, there has been a great amount of resources, time, energy, effort and commitment put into developing policy and initiatives to promote and develop physical activity and sporting opportunities for children in recent years. The PESSYP Strategy is the first national strategy of its kind and sees the largest financial investment in physical education and school sport ever made by government. Through its various programmes, it undoubtedly provides exciting opportunities for students, schools and teachers and the potential to really make a difference. Indeed, the outcomes of 'high quality' physical education and school sport which the Strategy endeavours to achieve and which young people should demonstrate have been defined and are as follows (our emphasis throughout):

◆ *are committed to physical education and sport and make them a central part of their lives – both in and out of school;*
◆ know and understand what they are trying to achieve and how to go about doing it;
◆ *understand that physical education and sport are an important part of a healthy, active lifestyle;*
◆ *have the confidence to get involved in physical education and sport;*
◆ have the skills and control that they need to take part in physical education and school sport;
◆ willingly take part in a range of competitive, creative and challenge-type activities both as individuals and as part of a team or group;
◆ think about what they are doing and make appropriate decisions for themselves;
◆ show a desire to improve and achieve in relation to their own abilities;
◆ *have the stamina, suppleness and strength to keep going;*
◆ *enjoy physical education, school and community sport.*

(DfES and DCMS 2004)

Thus, it would seem the PESSYP Strategy has the potential to increase children's participation and involvement in physical education, physical activity and sporting opportunities, as well as increase their enjoyment, confidence, and ultimately their fitness, health and well-being. Indeed, as highlighted in Chapter 2, the 2006/2007 School Sport Survey has revealed participation in at least two hours of physical education and school sport among schools in School Sport Partnerships to have increased from 62 per cent in 2003/04, to 86 per cent in 2006/07.

But, PESSYP aside, the number and range of other initiatives and organizations involved in promoting physical activity and sporting opportunities for children are also impressive and welcomed. All such opportunities, i.e. those provided by PESSYP and other organizations, need to be seized, capitalized upon, celebrated and most of all enjoyed! We should, however, not get too carried away and mislead you into thinking that such initiatives are and will be the solution to engaging all young people in physical activity. On a more cautionary note, we would like to make just a few general observations about them.

The nature of the initiatives

A number of the initiatives, and particularly those stemming from government policy and the PESSYP Strategy, focus primarily on the promotion and development of sport and sporting opportunities for youngsters. Relatively few promote lifetime physical activity and focus on more lifestyle, unstructured, or recreational activities (e.g. Safe Routes to School, Bike It, Jump Rope for Heart, Schools on the Move). Given that common barriers to children's participation in physical activity include perceptions that they are 'not the sporty type' and a dislike of the activities often offered to them (see Chapter 3), and that by free choice many children today are opting to take part in more lifestyle, non-competitive and recreational activities (see Chapter 8), it could be argued that these initiatives are unlikely to be attractive to *all* students, meet their needs and be of benefit. This point was also made in relation to the content of the physical education curriculum in Chapter 8.

Initiative overload?

Anecdotally, we would argue that many teachers are feeling bombarded with initiatives and resources. Therefore one could question whether we are at a point of initiative 'overload', as well as what impact these initiatives are likely to have. Personally, we welcome the range of initiatives and opportunities available but feel that teachers need to be selective and carefully consider how to select, manage and co-ordinate them to meet specific needs and physical activity goals. It would seem that there needs to be greater co-ordination of effort across government departments and the various organizations when developing and introducing initiatives. There are some good examples of successful collaboration and co-ordination (e.g. the Healthy Schools Programme; PESSYP). Indeed, the PESSYP Strategy is based on a strategic and co-ordinated approach within a national infrastructure for physical education and school sport. Furthermore, monitoring and evaluation of the PESSYP's programmes has been and continues to be carried out.

Targeted interventions

As noted in Chapter 10, because children are not a homogenous group, targeted interventions are recommended and calls have been made for interventions to be differentiated on the basis of gender, age and socio-economic status. Some of the initiatives we have outlined are differentiated and target the needs of specific groups (e.g. the Norwich Union GirlsActive (targeted at girls), and the Sky Living for Sport project (targeted at at risk youngsters)), though the majority are not.

Evaluation

In Chapter 11 we recommended that you evaluate the impact of any strategies you implement from the start and we gave you some monitoring and evaluation guidelines. It therefore seems ironic for us to report that only a few of these formal initiatives have been formally evaluated. Exceptions include the programmes that form part of the PESSYP Strategy and some of the Youth Sport Trust initiatives (e.g. TOPS and Sky Living for Sport). Due to a lack of or limited evaluation though, we know little about the effectiveness of many potentially valuable initiatives or their respective elements and the ways in which these influence children's lifestyles. This should not discourage you from getting involved and taking advantage of such initiatives, but it does mean that, until more widespread evidence is available, the design and delivery of effective initiatives will remain relatively uninformed, undirected and somewhat 'hit and miss'. In the same way, we know little about the impact or likely impact of the resources that are available.

Recommendations

When considering introducing, using and/or drawing ideas from any of these initiatives or resources in your school, the 'Practical tips for implementing strategies' which we highlighted in Chapter 11 also apply here. In addition though, we offer the following concluding recommendations.

◆ If possible, build formal initiatives into an Active School (or other school) Policy to be implemented by an Active School Committee – this will allow co-ordination, integration and prioritization.

- Before committing fully to any initiative, research it fully and establish exactly what it entails – ensure that it meets your students' needs and physical activity goal(s) and that you have adequate resources for implementation.
- Prepare thoroughly for the implementation of initiatives – 'by failing to prepare, you will be preparing to fail'.
- Organizations and initiatives at regional and local level can also support the promotion of physical activity. Try to establish which local organizations or partners could support the promotion of physical activity among students in your school.
- Linked to the above, try to establish any local programmes and initiatives that support the promotion of physical activity among children in your area.
- Familiarize yourself with the resources available and begin to build a bank of resources to support your efforts. Before using resources with students, evaluate their suitability for the particular group.
- Familiarize yourself with the useful contacts and access the organizations' websites. From the information provided, consider how each organization may be able to support you in the promotion of physical activity among your students (e.g. what service(s) does the organization provide and how might these be used/help?).
- Keep abreast of new initiatives, resources and developments by taking advantage of relevant professional development opportunities, reading professional journals and accessing relevant websites.

Concluding remarks

We wish you well in your efforts to promote physical activity, and ultimately in 'getting the buggers fit'. To this end, we hope that this book has inspired you and given you the knowledge, confidence and determination to be able to make a real difference to the physical education, physical activity experiences and physical activity levels of your students.

Reference

DfES and DCMS (2004), *High Quality PE and Sport for Young People. A Guide to Recognising and Achieving High Quality PE and Sport in Schools and Clubs*. London: DfES and DCMS.

Index

abnormal blood lipid levels 140
accelerometers 87, 88, 90
Achievement Motivation and Goal
    Orientations, Theory of 32, 33
achievement orientation 33, 38
active lifestyles 162
active play 18
Active School 156, 159–61
    committees 184–5
    policies 159
Active School Policy 171, 184
activities 104
    developmentally appropriate 55
    sedentary 21, 40
activity levels 22, 69, 91, 133
activity patterns 101
activity profiles 132
activity promotion 114
activity scores 87
activity weeks 161
activity-based units 117
adolescence 5, 9, 15, 33, 34, 136
adolescents 8, 21, 51, 162
    food intake 21
adulthood 13, 18, 26
adults 10, 22, 23, 42, 62, 131, 139
aerobic activities 144
aerobic dance 131
aerobic exercise 14, 142
aerobic fitness 13, 14, 15, 16, 17, 23,
    25, 26, 49, 59, 71, 72–5
    tests 72
aerobics 45, 117, 136
affective learning 70
AfPE *see* Association for Physical
    Education
age 33, 35, 132

age groups 15
Amateur Swimming Association 205
American College of Sports
    Medicine 43
ancillary staff 10
anthropometry 60
aqua aerobics 135
aquafit 136
archery 135
art 130
assessment 69, 188
    methods 102
Association for Physical Education
    (AfPE) 52, 68, 159, 199
    Health Position Paper 133
    'Physical Education and
        Childhood Obesity'
        (seminar) 148
asthma 140, 142
athletes 204
    elite 70
athletics 118
attainment, levels of 164
attendance 103, 187, 206
attitudes 4, 34
Australia 13, 60
Australian Health and Fitness
    Survey 14
authority 4

back pain 45, 49, 59, 75, 140, 144
ballroom dancing 135
basketball 20, 45, 189
behaviour 4, 189, 190, 206
    healthy 64
    sedentary 36
Benchmarking Excellence 204

Bike It 208, 216
bike riding 20
blood pressure 9, 64
    high 72
BMI *see* body mass index
body composition 7, 59, 60–61, 68,
    71
body fat 6
body fatness 25
body image 34, 37, 38
body image disorder 140
body management 144
body mass 16–17
body mass index (BMI) 33, 60, 138,
    139, 142, 143
    measuring children's 143
body size 37
body weight 21, 33, 71, 88
bone health 45
bone mineral destiny 45
bones 75
boys 13, 15, 18–19, 26, 139
British Association of Sport and
    Exercise Sciences 52
British Council 211
British Heart Foundation 145, 159,
    208, 211
    guidance 145
British Olympic Foundation 209

Campbell Survey on Well Being in
    Canada 14
Canada 13, 60
Canada Fitness Survey 13
cancer 72
car use, reducing 158
cardio-respiratory system 72
cardiovascular activity 53
cardiovascular disease (CVD) 8, 10,
    13, 25, 140
    risk 9
cardiovascular fitness 7, 144
cardiovascular health 9
cardiovascular system 91
carers 147, 158, 195
case studies 189–96
catching 52

changing rooms 167
charitable trusts 199
child care 165
childhood 6, 15, 18
childhood obesity 5, 18, 45, 50, 138–
    51
childhood overweight 50
children 51
Children, Schools and Families,
    Department for 20, 157, 200,
    201, 207
cholesterol levels 141
chronic disease risk factors 8, 13, 25
citizenship qualities 206
citizenship skills 194
class registers 167
climbing 52
Club Links 200, 203
clubs 189
    out of school hours 104
cognitive learning 70
colleagues 12
commercial organizations 199
community links 180–81
community partnerships 180–81
community sports 34
Competence Motivation Theory 32,
    33
competence orientation 33
competition 42
competition managers 46
competitive sport 123, 135
computer games 4, 21, 36, 37
concentration span 37
confidence 69, 102, 144
    lack of 36, 39
contacts 5, 211–14
Continued Professional
    Development 210
convenience foods 141
core messages 147
core subjects 122
coronary heart disease 50, 72, 121
correlates 29, 30, 31, 32, 33–4
    personal 32
    psychological 32
    social 32

critical thinking 102
cross-country running 42, 116, 117, 134
cultural pressures 37, 39
Culture, Media and Sport, Department for 20, 200
curriculum 7, 42, 67, 72, 92, 119, 121, 130, 156, 157, 159, 160–61, 186, 206
    health education 50
    hidden curriculum 157
    physical education 6, 30, 46, 66, 107–21, 122, 123, 135, 147, 155, 164, 166, 206
curriculum review 194
Curriculum 2000 113, 135
CVD *see* cardiovascular disease
cycle ergometers 14
cycling 20, 45, 50, 130, 131, 135, 141
cynicism 37
Czech Republic 15

dance 45, 118, 190
dancing 52
delivery 55, 119, 133
departmental policies 167, 172–6
departmental practices 172–6
depression 34, 140
Design and Technology 124, 130
desirable practices 120
determinants 29
diaries 187, 188
    physical activity 101
diet 140
    balanced 147
    healthy 34, 142
dietary behaviours 10–11
dietary habits 14
disabled 209
discomfort 36, 39
discrimination 140
distance runs 59
diving 20
Dreams + Teams 211
drinking 14
DVD watching 36, 37

eating disorders 143
eating habits 21
eating patterns 140
education 11
Education Act 1996 10
Education and Skills, Department for 201
educationalists 3
ego 33
elite athletes 70
embarrassment 36, 39, 144
emotional health 157
emotional well-being 157
endurance 7, 49, 59, 68, 71, 75–8
energy balance 141
Enfield, Harry 4
environment 56, 69, 147, 179
environmental factors 35, 156
equipment 69, 133
Estonia 15
ethnic differences 132
ethnic minorities 35, 165
ethnicity 33
Europe 15, 17, 60
evaluating skills 134
evaluation 55, 70, 168, 185–7
events 104
Every Child Matters 11, 115
examination results 122, 188
exercise 6, 18, 19, 34, 131, 190
    'hard' exercise 42
    health-related 6
    high-intensity 42
exercise effects 114
exercise tolerance 142, 144
exercise training 9
exercises
    differentiated 52
    stretching 53
Exeter University
    Children's Exercise and Health Research Centre 16
    study 22
extracurricular activities 19

facilities 50, 161
fast foods 141

fat 71, 141
fatness 3, 8, 13, 33
feedback 61, 63, 70
females 33
fencing 135
field tests 62
field-based studies 14
financial resources 37
fingerprint monitoring 143
Finland 15
fitness 3, 4, 41, 61–4, 66, 144, 215
  activities 118
  assessment 61
  cardiovascular 59, 68
  health-related 68, 71
  instructors 41
  levels 54, 65
  personal 70
  physical 86
  programmes 58
  regimes 42, 116
  scores 16
  studies 14
  test batteries 68
  test data 66
  test scores 67, 70
  tests 59–61, 67
fitness testing 17, 42, 58, 64–7, 68, 69, 71–80, 116, 134
  limitations 86
  methods 59–64
  process 69
  purposes of 64
  recommendations 67–70
FITNESSGRAM 69, 101
FITNESSGRAM/ ACTIVITYGRAM 61, 101
flat feet 144
flexibility 7, 45, 49, 51, 56, 59, 68, 71, 79–80
  training 51, 54
food, adolescents 21
football 20, 190
fractures 144
friendship groups 37
fruit 141
funding 201

Gaelic football 135
games 45, 118, 132
  team games 134, 135
games activities 108
gardening 6, 18, 48
gender 132
genetics 23, 62, 65
geography 130
Gifted and Talented 200, 203–4
  Physical Education Quality Standards 204
girls 13, 15, 18–19, 26, 30, 35, 37, 39, 136, 139, 143, 162, 165, 191–2, 217
  adolescent 38
goal setting 58, 69, 155
goals 43, 55, 166
gold medal winners 42
golf 135
government 122, 199,
  initiatives 200–207
  obesity target 142
  policies 115–16, 138
  strategies 200–207
government ministers 3
governors 10, 145, 157, 181, 185
guidelines 43
  'Children's Lifetime Physical Activity Model' 44
  curricular 61
  'Physical Activity Guidelines for Adolescents' 44
gymnastics 45, 52, 189
gyms 48

HEA *see* Health Education Authority
headteachers 145
health 3, 6, 11, 12, 16, 23, 34, 43, 46, 49, 66, 107, 113, 156, 215
  activities 118
  enhancement 116
  mental 139
  physical 139
health and fitness 42, 107, 166
health benefits 4, 7–10, 114
Health Development Agency 115

Health Education Authority
(HEA) 44, 51, 115, 161, 171
recommendations 48
health education, curriculum 50
health indicators 9
health messages 37
health practitioners 3
health problems 71
health professionals 51
health promotion 6
health risks 16
Health Survey for England 22
Health Survey for England (1997) 19
Health Survey for England
(2006) 18–19, 139
Health, Department of 145, 157,
207, 211
obesity guidance 147
health-based programmes 107
health-based work 123
health-related exercise (HRE) 6, 107,
113, 116–21, 122, 124–9, 133,
160
delivery 119
practice 123
working group 113
Health-Related Exercise in the National
Curriculum 113
Healthy Eating 157
Healthy Fitness Ranges 71
Healthy School 156, 157–9
Healthy School Status 159
Healthy Schools Physical Activity
Booklets 188
Healthy Schools Programme 147,
190–91, 216
heart conditions 71
heart disease 42
heart rate 48, 73
monitors 75, 89, 91
monitoring 87, 88, 91
height 37
heredity 62, 65
hidden curriculum 157
high-intensity exercise 42
history 130
hockey 136

Holmes, Dame Kelly 210
homework 165, 168
household chores 36, 165
housework 6, 18, 48
HRE *see* health-related exercise
hygiene issues 116
hypertension 8, 140

Iceland 15
identity 102
inactivity, risks 121
information gathering 185
initiatives 199, 216
injury 42
instructional materials 61
insulin resistance 8
insulin sensitivity 141
intensity 49
inter-house sport 194–6
internet, surfing 36
interviews 168, 186, 188
isolation 144–5
IT 130

JAE *see* Junior Athlete Education
jogging 131
joints 75
judo 135, 189
Jump Rope for Heart 208, 216
jumping 52
Junior Athlete Education (JAE)
programme 204
junk food 4

Key Stage 2 205
Key Stage 3 108, 124, 125–6, 135,
192, 193, 194
Key Stage 4 108, 124, 127–9, 135,
164, 165, 192, 193, 195
Key Stages 114

language 147
languages 130
leadership skills 194, 206
lean body mass 71
learning
affective 70

learning, *cont.*
  cognitive 70
  personalized 102
learning difficulties 140
learning opportunities 165
learning outcomes 113
legislation 6
leisure time 133
lessons 19, 20
lethargy 36
levels of attainment 164
lifestyle 9, 14, 62, 141
  lifestyle change 136
lifestyles 3, 4, 5, 21, 42, 65, 107, 133, 156
  active 41, 109, 110, 111, 112, 155, 162
  healthy 23, 41, 102, 109, 111, 112, 157, 206
  sedentary 18, 26, 29, 36
lifting 52, 53
ligaments 75
lipids 64
  lipid profile 8
lipoprotein profile 8
local authorities 158
Local Healthy School Programmes 158
Local Programmes 158
log books 188
low self-esteem 140
lunch boxes 143

males 33
management, senior 165, 185
mapping 130
mastery goals 33
mathematics 102
maturation 62, 64, 65
  maturational influences 23
media 3
  popular 12
media reports 3, 138
mental health 42, 139
  mental health problems 143
mental well-being 109, 111
metabolic profile 141

mile run test 66
mobility exercises 74
monitoring 185–7
moral development 8
mortality statistics 9
motivation 36, 62, 193–4
motor skills 102
movement efficiency 144
Multistage Fitness test 59, 61, 64, 72
muscles 75, 103
muscular endurance 59
muscular strength 7, 45, 49, 59, 68, 71, 75–8
musculo-skeletal system 75
music 76, 77, 130

National Audit Office 161
National Children and Youth Fitness Studies 13
National Curriculum 117, 125–6, 160, 192, 211
  requirements for health and fitness 113
National Curriculum for Physical Education (NCPE) 3, 86, 108, 113, 117, 123, 135
  terminology 135
  Wales 113
National Curriculum for Wales 113
National Dance Teachers Association 203
National Diet and Nutrition Survey 141
national fitness surveys 23
National Governing Bodies of Sport 204
National Healthy Schools Programme (NHSP) 157, 171, 195, 207
  website 159
National Healthy Schools Status 158
National Heart Forum 161
National Institute for Health and Clinical Excellence (NICE) 145, 161
  guidance 145–7
NCPE *see* National Curriculum for Physical Education

netball 136, 190
NHSP *see* National Healthy Schools
    Programme
NICE *see* National Institute for
    Health and Clinical Excellence
non-participation 144–5
Northern Ireland 13
Northern Ireland Fitness Survey 13
Norwich Union GirlsActive 210–11,
    217
    roadshows 210
obesity 3, 6, 8, 13, 18, 25, 42, 45, 72,
    121, 145, 147
    boys 139
    childhood 5, 50, 138–51
    contributory factors 140–41
    girls 139
    health problems 139–40
    measuring 139
    misclassification 139
obesity epidemic 138
observation 87, 88, 90, 92
orienteering 135
orthopaedic problems 144
osteoporosis 45, 49, 75
outcome expectations 34
outcomes 87, 206
out-of-hours school sport 20
overweight 8, 13, 45, 65, 134, 139,
    141, 147
    childhood 50

parent attitudes 166
parental support 34, 39
parents 4, 10, 12, 51, 70, 87, 147,
    157, 158, 165, 181, 185, 195
partnerships 201, 206
part-time work 165
PEA *see* Physical Education
    Association
pedometers 87, 88, 89, 91
peer groups 37
peer modelling 34
peer observations 168
peer support 34
peers 38
performance 66

performance goals 33
personal activity, knowledge 101–2
Personal and Social Education 113
Personal Best Challenge Parks 209–10
personal fitness 70
personal improvement 33, 53, 69
personal learning 186
Personal, Social and Health Education
    (PSHE) 124, 134, 157
    curriculum 108
personalized learning 102
PESS *see* Physical Education and
    School Sport
PESSCL *see* Physical Education,
    School Sport and Club Links
PESSYP *see* Physical Education,
    School Sport and Young
    People
physical activity 3, 4, 5, 6, 8, 10, 12,
    17, 18, 19, 21, 22, 23, 24, 29,
    31, 32–3, 34, 35, 36, 37, 38, 39,
    40, 41, 42, 43, 44, 45, 47, 48,
    50, 58, 65, 66, 67, 88, 91–101,
    103, 116, 117, 123, 131,
    133–6, 140, 141, 145, 155,
    157, 166, 171, 181–3
    behaviour 38
    determinants 132
    diaries 101
    government targets 45–7
    monitoring 87
    participation 164
    patterns 131
    policies 159
    programmes 142
    promotion 6, 160, 164, 188, 122
    recommendations 43–5, 46–7, 48,
        50, 51, 54, 55, 93, 102, 113,
        131
Physical Activity Guidance
    booklets 159, 171
Physical Activity Policy 184
physical competence 33, 38
physical education 4, 7, 10, 20, 34,
    41, 42, 45, 46, 91, 102, 113,
    119, 162, 168, 171, 188, 205
    curriculum 6, 7

physical education, *cont.*
  lessons 46
  teachers 10
Physical Education and School Sport
  (PESS)
  Investigation 206
  website 188
Physical Education and School Sport
  Professional Development
  programme 202
Physical Education Association
  (PEA) 68
Physical Education Matters 199
Physical Education, School Sport and
  Club Links (PESSCL)
  Strategy 45
physical education
  courses 124
  curriculum 30, 46, 66, 86,
    107–21, 122, 123, 135, 147,
    155, 164, 166, 206
  departments 165, 167
  health 123
  lessons 42, 88, 103, 116, 133,
    142, 145, 192
  National Curriculum for 108
  organizations 113
  policies 165
  programme 160
  teachers 3, 41, 107, 123, 149–51
'Physical Education and Childhood
  Obesity' (seminar) 148
  Strategy 45, 46, 202–3, 215, 216,
    217
Physical Education and Sport
  Strategy for Young People
  (PESSYP) 11, 20, 22, 115, 122,
    200–206, 216
physical fitness 5, 7, 10, 12, 16, 23,
  49, 67
  health benefits 7–10
  monitoring 86
  testing 67
physical health 139
physical well-being 109, 111
planning 55
planning skills 134

play 132
  equipment 205
playgrounds 156
  Zoneparc model 204–5
playing fields 156
Polar Sports tester 88
policies 168
poor exercise tolerance 142
portfolios 187
posture 52, 75, 140, 144
power walking 125
practitioners 22
President's Council on Physical
  Fitness 13
Primary Link Teachers 202
primary schools 20, 188, 202, 204
  children 143
professional development 200,
  202–3
Professional Development
  Managers 202
programme planning 155
PSHE *see* Personal, Social and Health
  Education
psychological distress 45
psychological problems 140
psychological well-being 8, 25, 141
puberty 5, 15
public health 44
Public Service Agreement 45

QCA *see* Qualifications and
  Curriculum Authority
  Physical Education and School
  Sport Investigation 201,
  205–6
  website 188, 205, 206
questionnaires 92, 93, 94–101, 168,
  186, 188, 191, 193, 194
  computer-based 101

range of movement 79
rebellion 37, 40
Record of Achievement (ROA) 101,
  103
recovery 74, 75
recreation 45, 135

rectus abdominis 76
reflection 136
registers 186, 188
report cards 61, 101, 143
research 49, 131–2
researchers 3, 20, 22, 91
resistance training 53
resource cards 209
resources 5, 37, 124, 133, 184, 199, 211–14, 215, 216
respect 56
respiratory problems 140
ROA *see* Record of Achievement
road user safety 158
role models 70
running 52, 73
   cross-country 116, 117, 134

Safe Routes to School 195, 207–11, 216
   website 208
safety 130
safety issues 114, 116
schemes of work 113
school ethos 176–8
school policies 145, 146, 162, 167, 172–6
school practices 172–6
school sport 7, 41, 46, 122, 168, 205
   sports days 21
School Sport Co-ordinators 158, 202
School Sport Partnership (SSP) 20, 46, 170, 200, 201–2, 204, 215
School Sport Survey 20–21, 215
School Travel Plan 158, 195, 208
schools 50, 107, 206, 215
   food policy 147
   primary 20, 188, 202, 204
   secondary 20, 188, 202
Schools on the Move 211, 216
Science 124
Second World War 107
Secondary National Curriculum for England 108
secondary schools 20, 188, 202
sedentary activities 21, 34, 40
sedentary behaviour 36

sedentary lifestyles 13, 18, 26, 29, 36
self-consciousness 36, 144
self-efficacy 32, 33, 34, 38
self-esteem 8, 144, 193
self-evaluation 69
   skills 102
self-management 155, 187
   skills 136
self-monitoring 58, 69, 101
self-reflection 168
self-reinforcement 155
self-reports 87, 89, 92
self-testing
   skills 58
senior management 4, 165, 185
sensation seeking 34
sex 35
siblings 34, 39
significant others 34
skateboarding 135
skeletal health 13, 25
skipping 45
Sky Living for Sport 210, 217
sleep apnoea 140
Slovakia 15
smoking 14
social activities 36
Social Cognitive Theory 32
social development 8
social group differences 132
social isolation 140
social pressures 32, 37, 39
social well-being 109, 111
socio-economic status 33
software 101
special schools 202
Specialist Schools Programme 201
Specialist Sports Colleges 200, 201, 202
specialist status 201
speed limits 208
sport 7, 18, 19, 20, 42, 45, 113, 131, 171
   competitive 123, 135
   inter-house 194–6
   organized 48
   promotional events 181–3

Sport England 19, 206–7
  Young People and Sport
    Survey 19, 22, 123
Sporting Champions 206–7
Sporting Playgrounds 200, 204–5
sports clubs 191, 207
sports coaches 41
Sports Colleges 201, 202
sports days 21, 161
sports facilities 36, 167
sports initiatives 166
Sports Leaders Award 193, 195, 209
Sports National Schools Population
  Survey 13
sports performers 42
sports practice 132
sports science, courses 124
SSP *see* School Sport Partnership
  redeploying 192–3
  support staff 184
  training needs 184
staff training 146
statutory requirements 3
step (exercise) 136
step counters *see* pedometers
Step into Sport 195, 200, 203, 209
straight abdominal muscle 75
strategies 183–4
street dancing 135
strength 51
  muscular 7
  training 51, 53
stretching exercises 53
striking 52
student attainment 166, 167
  assessment 186
student interviews 188
student performance
  assessment 186
Student Profiles 101
students 4, 12, 119, 157, 160, 181,
  210, 215
studies 15, 21
  international 17
  UK-based 17
sugar 141
support staff 184, 210

surveys 21
  national fitness 14
Sustrans 207, 208
swimming 20, 45, 135, 200, 205
Swimming and Water Safety,
  website 205
Swimming Charter 205
SWOT analysis 170, 171
synchronized swimming 135

table tennis 190
Taking Part Survey (2006) 20
Taking Part Survey (2007) 21
Talent Identification in Physical
  Education 204
target groups 30
target setting 168
task learning 33
Tate, Catherine 4
teacher assessments 189
teacher competence 67
teacher interviews 188
teacher knowledge 123–4
teacher observations 187, 188
teacher training 123
Teacher Training Agency *see*
  Training and Development
  Agency for Schools
teachers 10, 51, 86, 113, 119, 135,
  210, 215, 216
  new 124
  physical education 41, 107, 123,
  149–51
teaching assistants 10
teaching environment 186
teaching methods 186, 187
teaching strategies 166, 168
teaching styles 165, 166, 168, 186,
  187
team games 134, 135
team work 187
teenage years 15, 18
teenagers 26, 121, 131
television 4, 21, 36, 37
tendons 75
tennis 190
test batteries 61–4, 68

test manuals 61
tests 69
theory 117
Theory of Achievement Motivation
    and Goal Orientations 32, 33
Theory of Planned Behaviour 32
Theory of Reasoned Action 32
thinking skills 102, 186
throwing 52
time management 155
TOPS 217
    TOP Activity Programmes 209
    TOP Link 209
    TOP Play 209
    TOP Programmes 208–9
    TOP Sportsability 209
    TOP Start 209
    TOP Tots 209
Top-Up Swimming Toolkit 205
training 42
    'hard training' 42
Training and Development Agency
    for Schools 124
trampolining 189
transport 50, 132
transportation 45
travel patterns 21, 141
treadmills 14
trunk strength 45
type 2 diabetes 140

underachievers 35

United Kingdom 17, 120, 122, 139,
    161
United States of America 13, 16, 17,
    43, 60
units of work 113
USA *see* United States of America

vegetables 141
video games 36

walking 18, 45, 48, 50, 130, 135,
    141
water polo 135
websites 5, 211–14
weight 37
weight gain 141
weight management 42, 121
weight training 135
weights 53
well-being 43, 46, 156, 215
whole-school environment 145, 146
work commitments 49
World Health Organization 138

young adulthood 9
'Young and Active' 44, 115
young people 19, 35
Young People and Sport National
    Surveys 19, 123
Youth Dance England 203
Youth Sport Trust 171, 204, 208–9,
    211, 217